Negotiating
Graduate
School

To
Philip Rossman, M.D., 1905-1992
A quiet man of gentle strength: my father

Negotiating Graduate School

A Guide for Graduate Students

Mark H. Rossman

SAGE Publications
International Educational and Professional Publisher
Thousand Oaks   London   New Delhi

For information address:

SAGE Publications, Inc.
2455 Teller Road
Thousand Oaks, California 91320

SAGE Publications Ltd.
6 Bonhill Street
London EC2A 4PU
United Kingdom

SAGE Publications India Pvt. Ltd.
M-32 Market
Greater Kailash I
New Delhi 110 048 India

Printed in the United States of America

Library of Congress Cataloging-in-Publication Data

Rossman, Mark H., 1940–
    Negotiating graduate school : A guide for graduate students / Mark
H. Rossman.
        p.   cm.
    Includes bibliographical references.
    ISBN 0-8039-7114-1 (hard: alk. paper). — ISBN 0-8039-7115-X
(pbk.: alk. paper)
        1. Universities and colleges—Graduate work—Handbooks, manuals,
etc. 2. Dissertations, academic—Handbooks, manuals, etc.
I. Title.
LB2371.R67   1995
378.1'553—dc20   95-3258

This book is printed on acid-free paper.

95 96 97 98 99 10 9 8 7 6 5 4 3 2 1

Sage Production Editor: Gillian Dickens

Contents

Acknowledgments

A book of this type would not have been written had it not been for the success of the many graduate students I have worked with over the years at Walden University, Nova Southeastern University, Ottawa University, Arizona State University, and the University of Massachusetts. Thanks to you all.

Special acknowledgment is given to Dr. Gerald Rafferty. I served as his faculty adviser while he earned his Ph.D. Without his encouragement and assistance, I would not have written this book. Thanks, Gerald.

Thanks are also given to my editor, Mitch Allen. His keen eye kept me on the right track when I tended to stray.

I also want to acknowledge the unwavering support of my wife, Dr. Maxine Rossman, my children, Kim and Nicole, and my son-in-law, Marc.

Overview

The central theme of this book is that to succeed, graduate students need to be aware of the process of completing a graduate degree, control as many aspects of the process as possible, and be careful, skillful, and tactful negotiators. Simply stated, this book is designed to help students complete a graduate degree.

The author has worked exclusively with graduate students at the master's and doctoral level for more than 25 years. The book provides realistic answers to the questions and concerns most often raised by graduate students. It describes the process of completing a graduate degree, identifies relevant questions and concerns, and provides practical solutions and suggestions.

Chapter 1 addresses the uncertainties of many students in graduate school. This chapter helps the reader to clarify reasons for being in graduate school, describes possible barriers to success, and identifies positive motivators. It ends with a discussion of the need for support at work and at home. Chapter 2 provides useful information about developing and completing the program of study. Included is information regarding financing graduate education, selecting the right degree program, understanding the program of study, managing time, and controlling frustrations. Chapter 3 describes

1

the roles and functions of the members of the graduate committee, as well as how to know and be known by potential committee members, and provides a guide to use when selecting committee members. Chapter 4 describes the comprehensive examination—the written comp and the oral comp—as well as how to prepare for it and how to successfully complete it. Chapter 5 is a discussion of the proposal and how it connects to the thesis or dissertation. The content of each chapter in the proposal and of the thesis or dissertation is discussed. Chapter 6 helps the reader to understand, prepare for, and successfully complete the defense of the thesis or dissertation. The book ends with Chapter 7, in which practical suggestions are offered regarding what to do after completion of the degree.

ONE

Can I Really Complete a Graduate Degree?

When I completed my master's degree, I was sure I would never go back to school. Who would have believed it? Here I am working on my Ph.D.

My biggest fear was that I could not do the work. My advice to others is to take one step at a time. Don't look up and don't look back. Just look to see what you have to do today. Know when to ask for help and realize that this is part of the process.

Pat

Welcome to the world of graduate education. Reading this book is a good indication of your desire to earn a graduate degree. This won't be easy. You are in a world of the unknown and one that probably is just a little bit frightening.

You are not alone. In October 1993, the Council of Graduate Schools released the results of a survey that indicated that, in 1992, more than 1,130,000 people were enrolled in graduate school. About 54% of that number were women, and about 53% of the total were enrolled on a part-time basis. In 1992, more than 330,000 individuals earned their master's degree while about 39,000 earned a doctorate.

Many learners seeking a master's have some lingering doubts about their reasons for wanting a degree, their current scholastic abilities, and the impact graduate school will have on their families, their jobs, and their way of life. Although we are not supposed to admit it, many are frightened of what lies ahead.

There is, however, much joy and excitement associated with completing a graduate degree. In addition to promotions, higher salaries, and new job responsibilities, gratification is felt after working hard and completing an objective. A sense of personal accomplishment also accompanies the completion of a degree that, for many, has been a distant dream.

How This Book Can Help You

In this chapter, many of the questions and concerns raised by new and seasoned graduate students are identified. Exercises presenting ways of determining appropriate individual answers are provided. When finished with this chapter, the reader should have a much better understanding of some of the common concerns that face many individuals seeking a graduate degree as well as more control over the situation. Students will be in a much better position to forge ahead with confidence and join countless others of all ages and from many different backgrounds who are completing master's and doctoral degrees each year. They are doing it! So can you!

Chapter 2 describes how to develop and complete the graduate program of study. This chapter provides information on financing graduate school; understanding the different types of graduate degree programs; selecting and developing courses that meet program requirements as well as personal goals; managing time; understanding the relationship of the mind, body, and spirit to the completion of a graduate program; controlling frustrations; and understanding the changing roles of family, friends, and others.

It is vital to understand the relationship of the graduate committee to success as a graduate student. In Chapter 3, the obvious and subtle functions and roles of the committee are discussed. Techniques for becoming known by potential committee members and choosing an effective committee are provided.

Chapter 4 discusses the comprehensive examination. In this chapter, the purposes and components of the comprehensive exam are presented. Ways of preparing for it are explored. Several specific techniques for successfully completing both the oral and the written parts of the exam are provided.

The completion of a thesis or dissertation is what essentially differentiates an undergraduate from a graduate program. This is the focus of Chapter 5. Critical to the development of the thesis or dissertation is a well-designed proposal. This chapter helps the reader to understand and successfully use the proposal to guide the development of the thesis or dissertation and also presents tips and techniques about the parts of each chapter of the thesis or dissertation.

Defending the thesis or dissertation is the focus of Chapter 6. This chapter explains what is expected at a defense and provides several strategies for successfully completing it.

Chapter 7 contains information regarding what to do after the completion of the degree. Included is advice on how to use the time previously dedicated to program completion, binding the thesis or dissertation, copyrighting it, making it available for use by others, attending commencement, finding a job, publishing, and other suggestions designed to take advantage of the newly earned graduate degree.

The book ends with references and a list of general style guides; guides to writing a proposal, thesis, dissertation, or research paper; and guides to researching and writing in the disciplines.

Why Am I in Graduate School?

If 50 graduate students seeking to earn a graduate degree were gathered together and asked to list one reason they were in grad school, a list with 50 different reasons probably would result. Many might speak of their desire to reach a personal goal, such as completing the degree for no reason other than that they want it. Or the need to comply with licensing requirements or other requisites for keeping or obtaining a job is a motivation. Others may speak about the desire to learn something new or, simply, the desire to know. Still others may speak of vague needs for personal fulfillment or the need to take part in a social activity, make new friends, or move on after experiencing a life transition.

Three Categories of Learners

At least three basic categories are used to describe individuals who participate in educational activities:

- *Goal oriented*—those who are motivated to accomplish a specific goal or a clear-cut objective
- *Learning oriented*—those who are motivated to seek knowledge "for the sake of knowledge"
- *Activity oriented*—those who are motivated by the need for social interaction

It is not possible always to be in one category. But one's dominant category depends on a number of factors such as what is being offered, when it is being offered, how much it costs, or the length of time of the experience. Knowing something about the characteristics of the different types of learners is helpful when thinking about individual motivation and how this fits in with graduate education.

Those who fall most frequently into the *goal-oriented* category are generally impatient and believe that knowledge must be put to immediate use. They believe that pursuit of a purpose or objective is the primary motivation for obtaining a graduate degree. Learners in this category may experience difficulty with survey or introductory courses or those that are philosophical in nature because these courses tend to provide generalities or overviews while the goal-oriented learner tends to want specifics.

Many professors in traditional graduate schools lecture and give all they know about a particular subject. They frequently ramble and go off on seemingly unrelated tangents. A goal-oriented learner may find this difficult to cope with because this is not the preferred pattern of this type of learner.

The goal-oriented learner wants to see the immediate relevance of the information being presented and is frequently thinking: "*So what! How does this affect me?*" Regardless of a learner's dominant category, these seven words can help with applying the information to the job or resolving a personal problem or concern. How does the experience relate to you today and tomorrow? How does it relate to your job, your home life, your self-development, or the world around you? Asking yourself these questions or asking them of friends, family, colleagues, or professors can help make the information or experience more personally meaningful.

The *learning-oriented* learner is one who seeks knowledge for the sake of knowledge. These individuals are usually avid readers who see education as a constant, lifelong activity rather than occurring as an episodic activity. This type of learner fits in most closely with the philosophy of most graduate schools because their motivational patterns are most closely in tune with the ways in which graduate schools are set up.

This type of learner loves bibliographies and wants to know the genesis of each idea, all the various writers who have written on the subject, and all directly and indirectly related concepts, theories, constructs, or viewpoints. It is no wonder that this type of learner is a professor's dream.

The *activity-oriented* learner is frequently more in need of socialization and is seeking education more to fulfill this need than to acquire knowledge. Many times education may be used as an escape. This type of learner also may find graduate school more difficult than anticipated because socialization is not the main purpose of any graduate program.

This is not to say that unless you are learning oriented you won't succeed in graduate school. It simply points out that the philosophy of most graduate schools more easily facilitates the learning-oriented learner.

Many people who have earned their master's or doctoral degree consider themselves very practical people who have very clear-cut objectives, do not want to waste time on unnecessary activities, love to socialize, and don't see themselves as being particularly "learning oriented." Individuals such as these provide ample evidence of the two absolutely necessary attributes needed to complete anything in life: *drive* and *motivation.* With these attributes, almost anything is possible regardless of your dominant learning pattern. Without them, most things are more difficult.

The following activity is designed to help identify personal reasons for wanting a degree. To discover your own reasons, complete the following exercise:

Reasons for Wanting
a Graduate Degree

Directions: 1. In the space *immediately after* the letters below, list the reasons you can think of for wanting a graduate degree. Be as specific as possible—that is, to be promoted to manager, to gain more information related to your interests in self-education, to be able to change careers, and so on. It might help to think of what you want to be doing 5 years from now in terms of professional and personal aspirations.

   a.

   b.

   c.

   d.

   e.

2. Go back to the reasons you gave for wanting a graduate degree and, in the blank *before* the letters, label each reason with either an (E) if it is *employment* related or a (P) if it is *personal* and not employment related.

Discussion: Many people have a variety of reasons for wanting to return to school. None is better than another. However, it is important to think about and identify your reasons and motivation for desiring a graduate degree. Once you have completed this exercise, you should have a clearer idea of some of the real reasons why you want to complete your degree.

Motivation

How does motivation relate to success in grad school? It is possible that you may be experiencing a little bit of doubt about your success. How do you compare with your fellow learners? Why are you feeling a bit concerned about being able to succeed when you know you have succeeded in a variety of ways in the past? Although the desire to earn a graduate degree is strong, concerns or fears about the unknown may be preventing you from achieving your goals. This is a classical *approach-avoidance* situation. Knowledge of what may be happening can provide the needed motivation to move forward. You will be in a better position to take charge and control the situation rather than have it control you.

All people are motivated by drives. There are primary, innate drives such as hunger and thirst. And there are secondary drives such as desire, ambition, and fear. All drives are triggered by cues, which are little reminders that we have associated with our drives. Motivation is a result of having acquired a drive to attain a goal. The closer one gets to the goal, the more cues are present, and the greater is one's drive.

Cues can be negative and/or positive depending on the situation. A runner's drive increases closer to the finish line. The tape is in view, the crowd is roaring, the footsteps of other runners are heard in the background. The closer the runner gets to the finish line, the more powerful are the cues and the greater is the drive. But if the runner has on many occasions faltered at the point of victory, many of those same cues would become negative and serve as reminders of fear of past failures—the more similar this would be to the other races that had been lost and the greater would be the fear of failure.

Drives are triggered by cues. The same cue can be both negative and positive depending on how it is perceived by the individual. You may want to achieve a graduate degree and have the drive to achieve but you may also be avoiding it because fear of past failures, real or imagined, may be preventing you from starting or taking action to accomplish your goals. When the strength of the fear drive is stronger than the drive to achieve, action paralysis is in effect and movement toward earning the degree stops. Fear is stronger than the desire to achieve.

The following is designed to identify those cues that serve as positive motivators for you. Complete this exercise now.

My Positive Motivators

Directions: This activity is a two-part process. (a) In the spaces that follow, list all the reasons you can think of relating to why you want to earn a graduate degree and list them in the appropriate column. Reasons can be personal (e.g., "I want it to complete my education" or "I will feel more complete as an educated person with the degree") or they can be professional (e.g., "I need it for my promotion" or "I will be a more viable consultant if I have it"). (b) Once you have completed part 1, check with family, friends, and anyone else who knows you well enough to be able to suggest additional motivators. Add them to the list.

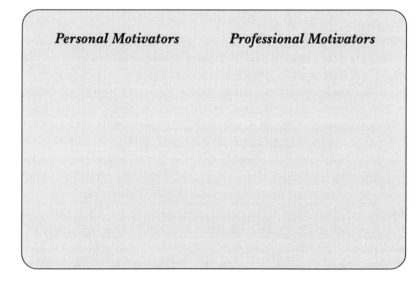

Personal Motivators   *Professional Motivators*

Discussion: When this list is completed, it will serve as a visual reminder of the motivators encouraging you to complete your degree. Post the list in several conspicuous places. This could be on the bulletin board in your home work space, in your office, next to your computer, in your notebook, above your bed, on the refrigerator, or anywhere else you will constantly see it. The more visible the list, the more often it will be seen and serve as a motivator to help you complete your graduate degree.

Barriers to Learning

We are not as good at identifying those things that are fear producing. What are some of the obstacles that may be preventing success?

K. Patricia Cross is a leading researcher on adult learning and the author of *Adults as Learners,* published in 1982. In her book, she talks about many of the barriers preventing learners from succeeding. Fears are imbedded in these barriers. Cross feels most, if not all, barriers to learning can be grouped under one of three headings: situational barriers, institutional barriers, or dispositional barriers. She defines them as follows:

1. *Situational barriers* are those arising from one's situation in life at a given time. Examples are lack of funds, childcare facilities, and transportation or lack of support from one's family or employer.
2. *Institutional barriers* are those practices and procedures that exclude or discourage individuals from participating in educational activities. Examples are inconvenient schedules or locations, full-time fees for part-time study, majors that don't reflect one's interests, or professors who fail to understand the needs of their students.
3. *Dispositional barriers* are those related to attitudes and self-perception about oneself as a learner. Examples are that you feel you really don't like to read and study or that you feel that you can't keep up with your fellow graduate students.

It is important to identify personally perceived barriers or obstacles that may prevent your success in graduate school. The following is an activity to assist with this.

My Barriers to Learning

Directions: This activity is a two-part process. (a) Think about your life in terms of the *situational, institutional,* or *dispositional* barriers (or obstacles) that may be preventing your success in graduate school. Keep in mind that barriers may be individually defined. What may be a barrier for one may not be a barrier for another. List all the barriers you can think of in the spaces provided. You do not have to fill in all the spaces. (b) Discuss this list with others who know you well to see if they can help identify additional barriers. Add the additional barriers to the list.

Situational Barriers (those arising from your current life situation):

1.
2.
3.
4.
5.
6.
7.
8.
9.
10.

Institutional Barriers (those practices and procedures you think are in place that exclude you or discourage you from participating in graduate school):

1.
2.
3.
4.
5.
6.
7.
8.

9.

10.

Dispositional Barriers (those personal attitudes and perceptions about yourself that you feel would prevent you from participating in graduate school):

1.

2.

3.

4.

5.

6.

7.

8.

9.

10.

Discussion: The purpose of this activity is to identify the fears and barriers that may be preventing you from getting started or making progress on your graduate degree. Simply identifying them is not enough. Action needs to be taken to eliminate them. Look at the source of the problem. Do you have the power to change or control it? How can it be modified? Many of the situational and dispositional barriers are ones over which a great deal of personal control is possible because they frequently are problems related to an attitude you hold about yourself or your circumstances. You can choose to do things differently, such as not feeling guilty for changing the family routine while you are in graduate school. You have the power to eliminate barriers to success. Take action!

Need for Support

Completion of a graduate degree requires the support of those around you. This includes family, friends, coworkers, and employer.

Perhaps most important in this process is family. You need to fully discuss your plans, thoughts, fears, and hopes with them. Share as much as you can about your reasons for being in school. Help them to know how important it is. Make sure all concerned know that there will be many changes in the time you can give to children or parents.

Many current patterns will need to be changed for you to be successful. Like most people in graduate school, you are or will be working either as a research assistant or as a teaching assistant or will be gainfully employed off campus. It is common to be concerned about finding the time to go to class, read the assignments, prepare for tests, and write term papers. You probably haven't even begun to think about all the time and effort required for the thesis or dissertation.

It is doubtful that you can continue to do all things at the same level of intensity at which you are now doing them. Something has to give. New ways will need to be found to complete responsibilities at work and at home. One way is to openly discuss concerns with those directly involved, that is, family, friends, and coworkers.

Work

Your work situation may need to change as the result of being in graduate school. The impact of graduate school on employment needs to be seriously considered. If you intend to remain employed while working on your degree and are worried about finding the time to do both and to do them well, openly discuss this with your employer. Developing solutions before anticipated problems become serious provides for greater control of the situation. Consider the following: Will you be able to continue to work full-time? Can you work part-time? Is a 4-day workweek an option? Can you afford to quit your job and live off loans or teaching or research assistantships?

Perhaps you will not be able to fully anticipate just what changes will be needed at work. To more fully understand what is expected, talk with coworkers or others who have completed a graduate degree in situations similar to yours. This will help identify possible problems.

Once you have some idea of the changes that are anticipated at work, discuss them fully with your employer. Perhaps a flextime arrangement in which you come to work early, stay late, or work at home or on weekends might provide the flexibility needed to attend classes during the day. Changing to a later shift might also work. Job sharing, a type of arrangement in which two people share one job, is another option. Remember, the worst that can happen is that the work situation cannot be changed. If this is so, and you need to earn money while in school, changing your current employment may be the only option.

Family

At home, someone will have to either take over or take on a greater share of your responsibilities. If this person is your mate, don't assume that he or she fully knows all that you do and knows what parts of your responsibility you want to give up, share, or keep. This person is not a mind reader. Full and frank discussions will be needed.

If you really think about it, going to graduate school isn't easy for either of you. After all, your mate's lifestyle is changing as well. Perhaps he or she will need to spend more time with the children while you study. Perhaps he or she will need to assume more of the housekeeping chores such as doing the laundry, mowing the lawn, or changing the lightbulbs. Everyone, including children, grand-children, and parents, needs to have a clear understanding of what changes will take place and what this means to established routines.

If cleaning and cooking are your major responsibilities, discuss available options. Could someone come in once a week to clean the house? Could your mate take this on? Are the children able to pitch in? Fast-food outlets are one way to relieve the cooking chores.

Open and honest communication is important. A frequent com-plaint of those with families who have returned to graduate school is that they really didn't know how many changes would be needed to complete their degree. They didn't realize the extent to which family routines would be disrupted. Realistically, weekends are not much fun for anyone when all you want to do is find time to study rather than go to a movie or to a restaurant. No matter how much support may be promised, when you are actually fully involved with working on your degree, it is often difficult for families to deal with it.

There is no easy solution to this dilemma. A good suggestion is to continually discuss concerns and feelings. All involved need to make concessions at various times. Each person needs to give a little and know when to back off. It also helps when all are learning, progressing, and recognizing the accomplishments of one another.

Try not to become so absorbed in your program that you trivialize or, worse, don't acknowledge the accomplishments of your mate or children.

Parents, siblings, and in-laws need to be included when planning the successful completion of your graduate degree. To what extent are they able to help out? Don't assume that your parents are built-in baby-sitters.

It is not uncommon for extended families to get together on weekends and holidays. Thanksgiving dinner with one set of parents and Christmas dinner with the other set is a tradition in many families. Grandparents look forward to visiting with the grandchildren. Although these visits are important in maintaining good, long-term family relationships, the weeklong annual get-together may not be possible while you are in graduate school. Phone calls may need to be temporarily curtailed or shortened.

Many times, family members, particularly parents and in-laws, don't realize all that is involved in earning a graduate degree and feel left out when the visits stop or the phone calls aren't made as regularly as usual. Let them know very early on that you are working to improve your future and that the disruptions are only temporary. It is not easy to cut down on the things that are enjoyable or that bring joy to others.

Perhaps it might help to remember that the more time expended in completing the degree, the sooner it will be done and life can return to normal.

Most who have successfully completed a graduate degree would agree that it is very helpful to be in a supportive environment. This also implies a need to interact with individuals who know, understand, and accept the pressures you are under. Family, friends, and fellow students are very important in this regard. Often students form support groups to provide this support. This is discussed more fully in Chapter 4.

Supporters, Detractors, and In-Betweeners

> *Supporters:* Those who support your graduate school plans
>
> *Detractors:* Those who are against your graduate school plans
>
> *In-Betweeners:* Those whose words or actions make it difficult to know if they are for or against your graduate school plans

As related to success in graduate school, the comments and actions of most family, friends, employers, and colleagues generally can be categorized by the ways in which they either help or hinder progress. Individuals who are in favor of what you are doing are supporters. Those who are against you are detractors. Sometimes it is difficult to determine if a person is a supporter or a detractor. These are in-betweeners.

Supporters. Supporters may be friends, colleagues, or family members who provide constructive criticism or who challenge you to strive for greater accomplishments. They show support through words of encouragement, sensitivity to the need for study time, or action to take over household chores that you have done in the past. These individuals may also be faculty members, mentors, or other role models who provide sage advice as well as assistance.

Detractors. Some people do not want you to succeed. They may be envious or jealous of you. Whatever their reasons, they drain your energy and can make life difficult.

They may be ambitious fellow students who take every opportunity to belittle you and other graduate students. Their techniques can be subtle but they frequently seek to build themselves up in the eyes of the professor by devaluing your contributions in class or by capitalizing on incorrect responses to questions posed by the professor. Rather than trying to understand them, the best advice is to avoid them.

17

In-Betweeners. Some people, especially family, like you just the way you are and do not really look forward to the changes that will occur after graduation. They may be just a bit apprehensive about your future plans or they may simply not adapt well to change. Their words or actions convey neither support nor opposition.

It is common for in-betweeners not to volunteer an opinion or to express it when asked. Frequently they don't want to offer their opinion because it might seem to be contrary to the new direction in your life or they may not want to express a counteropinion because they want to avoid a possible confrontation. When a decision has been made, they are fairly passive and do what they have to with little or no enthusiasm. It is difficult to determine any hidden meanings from their words or actions.

It might be useful to think about how to deal with each type of person as this will help ensure that maximum benefit from supporters will be obtained and that the negative force of the detractors and in-betweeners will be neutralized.

Going to graduate school demands much of you and those around you. It will not be easy and it will not be more of the same in terms of undergraduate work. It is a challenging prospect, especially if it has been a while since you were last in school. However, keep in mind that things have changed. You have changed. By carefully looking at the reasons you want a graduate degree and taking care to rearrange your life to be able to take on this new responsibility, you will be able to make it. Don't be afraid. Go for it!

TWO

The Program of Study

In my job, it is necessary to get a graduate degree in order to maintain my credibility. I never believed I could complete a program of study and still perform my professional responsibilities well. Besides, I never scored well of standardized tests and the GRE was an admission requirement for the program I was interested in.

After much coaxing, I took the GRE and was admitted. I'm not spending as much time as I want with my family and I can't spend the weekend watching football or my favorite sitcoms. But it feels so good to be accomplishing my educational goals. My self-respect and my credibility have never been greater.

Fred

A recurring theme throughout this book is the need to negotiate and be in control as much as possible of every part of the graduate process. No one cares more about your success than you do.

In this chapter, developing and completing the program of study are discussed. Specific information, activities, suggestions, and tips about financing your degree, the many different types of degree programs, credits required for graduation, different types of courses, program development, course completion, time management, the relationship of the mind, body, and spirit to program completion, and controlling frustration are presented.

Financing Your Graduate Degree

Very few graduate students can completely finance their programs without some type of assistance. Most students pay for their education through a variety of sources such as personal savings or investments, tuition reimbursement programs from employers, gifts or loans from parents and family, various state and federal loans, scholarships, assistantships, grants, gifts and/or loans from the university or college, or other sources such as private foundations (of which there are hundreds) or philanthropic organizations.

Savings and Investments

Many feel the best way to finance an education is to use savings or investment funds. Although this may seem to make sense, some financial advisers insist that it makes more sense to borrow rather than to deplete savings accounts or liquidate investments. If you are considering withdrawing funds from savings or selling investments to finance your graduate education, be advised to consult with a financial adviser regarding the best way to secure the necessary funds.

University or College Sources

When it comes to financing education, the most knowledgeable person on campus is the college or university financial aid officer. Get to know him or her soon because this person is aware of various sources of funding specific to your university and can provide good advice regarding current federal loan programs and other possible sources of money such as scholarships or grants from college or university sources.

However, don't rely totally on financial aid personnel because there are several sources such as grants from foundations with specific purposes that the financial aid officer may not be aware of. For example, if you are Polish, be aware of the Kosciuszko Foundation in New York City. This foundation provides financial assistance to full-time graduate and postgraduate students of Polish background who are U.S. citizens or permanent residents. It also provides assistance to Americans who are not of Polish extraction but are interested in studying Polish subjects. Students lose some control of the process when they assume that the people in the financial aid office know everything about them and their interests.

A common source of financial assistance for graduate students is through a teaching assistantship (TA) or a research assistantship (RA). Basically, a TA requires the recipient to teach in return for money and/or benefits such as reduced tuition or medical coverage. RAs are more nebulous but generally require the recipient to engage in research, usually on a professor's research project.

An intangible benefit of both types of assistantships is that recipients become known by the professors and get to know the professors as well. This is helpful when selecting committee members. More will be said about this in Chapter 4.

Be sure to personally check with the department or college for departmental grants and teaching and/or research assistantships because these may not be as well known to the financial aid office as they are within your graduate department.

Federal Sources

Unlike the undergraduate experience, there are no federal grant programs for graduate students such as the Pell Grant or Supplemental Education Opportunity Grant Program. For the most part, the federal government has replaced grants with loans as the primary source of money to graduate students. When considering loans, realize that most need to be paid back shortly after graduation or when you are no longer enrolled in a degree program. Learners enrolled in graduate programs can borrow, usually at competitive interest rates, from the following federal sources:

- Carl D. Perkins Loan Program
- Parent Loans for Undergraduate Students (PLUS) Program (yes, this program is for graduate students despite its name)
- Stafford Student Loan (SSL) Program
- Supplemental Loan for Students (SLS) Program

Don't assume that, having been denied a loan as an undergraduate, you will be denied again as a graduate student. At the graduate level, financial aid is based on a different set of criteria. Because there is much detailed paperwork regarding federal financial aid, it is essential to work closely with the financial aid office to be aware of the timetables, forms to be completed, and other regulations affecting the loan process.

Perhaps the most comprehensive source of federal money for graduate students is available by writing to the United States Department of Education, Washington, DC 20202. Ask for a complete description of all programs that may be of interest to you. When you write, be sure to include as much information about your degree program, interests, and needs as this makes the response easier and more meaningful.

State Sources

Financial assistance is available from a variety of state sources as well. Usually, the student needs to be a resident of the state to receive state funds. As individual state requirements vary, it is advisable to contact the financial aid person in your state department of education and ask about loans or grants available to graduate students. Many state departments of education maintain a library that contains a variety of sources of aid. If possible, make a trip to the state department of education and meet with the financial aid person. While there, be sure to look for any other state, federal, private, or public sources that may provide assistance.

Family

Parents and family are another good source of financial assistance. Often it is easier to get a loan or a gift of money from parents or family than from any other source. It makes good sense to treat this source of funds as you would any other. This means fully discussing your needs, the amount needed, and repayment terms. Recognize, too, that just because funds are needed to finance your degree, this may not be a sufficient reason for family to provide it.

Younger graduate students may not realize that as parents age, they often feel a greater need to provide for their own future and, with the best of intentions, may not be able or willing to provide additional funds for your graduate degree.

Employers

Many employers have tuition reimbursement programs or other company funds available to pay college costs. These programs frequently provide funds for graduate students because the company generally recognizes the ultimate benefit not only to you but also to the company. As many of these programs are private and vary in terms of how much is available, repayment terms, and other qualifications, you are well advised to speak with the personnel office of your company to learn if your company has funds of this nature and if they are available to you. If they do not, it might make sense to request financial assistance from your employer, stressing the advantages to both you and the company.

There are many books and articles available to graduate students seeking financial aid. At the end of this chapter is a list of several such publications. These are usually available through local and university libraries. It is difficult to discover all the many sources of aid that are available. But just like anything else, the more you are aware of potential sources of assistance, the more you control the process.

Am I in the Right Graduate Degree Program?

Before we discuss the parts of the program of study, you need to be sure you are in the right graduate degree program. This becomes all the more important with the realization that, throughout the world, more than 120 varieties of master of arts (M.A.) degrees and 270 varieties of master of science (M.S.) degrees are offered by more than 350 colleges and universities. In the United States alone, almost 300 *different* graduate degrees have been awarded by accredited colleges or universities. This doesn't include the different types of professional degrees such as master of education, master of business administration, master of music, and master of fine arts. It also doesn't include all the different types of doctoral degrees.

A careful reading of the graduate catalogue will reveal that the degree is awarded upon the recommendation of the faculty offering the graduate degree. Policy guidelines offered by the Council of Graduate Schools of the United States (1991) suggest that graduate degrees should be characterized as being primarily research oriented or professionally oriented. The degree is usually defined by a specific *degree title,* that is, master of arts (M.A.), master of business administration (M.B.A.), master of science (M.S.), doctor of philosophy (Ph.D.), doctor of education (Ed.D.), and so on and a *specialization* (often referred to as a major or concentration). It makes sense to know the exact degree title and specialization before developing the program of study. Verify in advance that you are working toward a Ph.D. with a specialization in clinical psychology or an M.A. with a specialization in elementary education rather than *assuming* that this is the degree and specialization to be awarded upon graduation.

Occasionally professional degrees such as the educational specialist (Ed.S.) or the certificate of advanced graduate studies (C.A.G.S.) fit between the master's and the doctorate. It sometimes is not clear or obvious if these are degrees or certificates. In some cases, the university or college grants one as a degree with the same full rights and privileges attached to any other graduate degree. In others, the college or university grants a certificate that certifies completion of a prescribed program of study but is not an earned degree. It is very important to check with the graduate school to be sure you are enrolled in the correct degree and specialization or major.

Defining the
Program of Study

To make the correct decisions about the program of study, it might be helpful to think about it in terms of academic credits.

CREDITS REQUIRED
FOR COMPLETING GRADUATE DEGREES

Type of Degree	Number of Credits
Master's degree (i.e., M.A., M.S.)	30-36
"Terminal" master's (i.e., M.B.A., M.S.W.)	60
Doctorate (i.e., Ph.D., Ed.D.)	90

Although programs vary regarding the number of credits required for a master's or doctoral degree, a general rule to follow is that a master's degree requires completion of from 30 to 36 credit hours. Exceptions to this rule are those master's degrees that are considered "terminal." These may require 60 or more graduate credits to complete. Examples of terminal degrees are the master of social work (M.S.W.) or the master of counseling (M.C.) degrees. The doctorate, including the dissertation, usually requires about 90 credits.

TIME REQUIRED TO
COMPLETE GRADUATE DEGREES

Master's degree (30-36 credits)	1 year
"Terminal" master's (60 credits)	2 years
Doctorate (90 credits)	3 years

Another way is to think that a minimum of 1 year of full-time post-baccalaureate study is generally required to complete the master's degree. Terminal master's degrees (i.e., M.S.W. or M.B.A.) usually require a minimum of 2 years of full-time study. To complete the doctoral degree usually requires a minimum of 3 of years full-time study.

Ideally, the graduate school has designed its graduate degree programs to reflect its own mission. The mission of the graduate program as well as its goals and objectives are usually described in the mission, goals, and/or purpose sections of the graduate school catalogue. The various degrees offered by the institution should clearly relate to the mission of the graduate school and/or department. Most graduate colleges or departments implement the mission and purpose through their graduate degrees and programs of study.

In many schools, the program of study is a predetermined series of courses followed by a comprehensive examination or other culminating experience such as a thesis, dissertation, or other research or applied research project. Although most doctoral degree programs require a dissertation of some sort, it is common for many master's degree programs not to have a thesis or any other final experience (see Chapters 4, 5, and 6 for more information on the comprehensive exam, thesis, and dissertation).

The following are the different types of courses that are common in most graduate programs:

- *Foundation or core* (usually required of everyone in the program)
- *Specialization* (usually required for specializations or majors)
- *Electives*
- *Field experience* (practicum or internship)
- *Independent study* (individualized, one-on-one study)
- *Thesis/dissertation*

It is frequently the norm for graduate programs to require that all graduate students in the department, regardless of their major or concentration, take a series of foundation courses known as the core. The thinking behind this usually is that the faculty want to be assured that every student has been exposed to a common base of knowledge as it relates to certain core concepts, principles, or ideas. An example would be a college of education requiring everyone at the master's level to take such courses as "The History and Philosophy of Education," "Introduction to Research," and "Field Experience" (sometimes called *practicum* or *internship*) regardless of the concentration area selected. This ensures that everyone completing a program of study in the college has at least been exposed to a common set of assumptions, knowledge, and literature related to the background and principles of education and research and will have an opportunity to apply information gained from the program of study in a "real-life" setting.

The scope and sequence of core courses or experiences usually have been developed by the faculty to reflect areas they believe are important. These courses frequently begin with an overview and are designed to provide breadth of information. These are usually the largest courses in the department because all students in the department are required to take them.

Core courses at the doctoral level are usually more advanced than those required at the master's level. At the doctoral level, faculty usually want to guarantee that the student has more in-depth exposure to basic knowledge, particularly as applied to research and/or other core requirements of the field or discipline. Although it is common for master's degree programs to require at least one course in statistics and another in research design, it is equally common for doctoral programs to require at least 9 to 15 credits to be taken in research and statistics as well as additional foundation and advanced courses in the discipline or field in addition to a practicum or internship experience.

In addition to core courses, a program of study usually consists of additional courses or experiences relating to the concentration or area(s) of specialization offered by the graduate program. These courses are frequently referred to as the "major" or "specialization" courses. Many graduate programs consider a major or specialization to be somewhere between 21 to 24 credits.

The purpose of these courses is to provide the latest and most current information about specializations offered by the college or department. These courses usually are more focused and frequently follow a seminar format in which there is frequent discussion among and between the professor and the class members.

The field experience (practicum or internship) is designed to provide a "hands-on" opportunity to apply information gained through coursework or to acquire specific information needed to complete a specialization area. These are usually completed "on site" and involve a local on-site supervisor cooperating with the university professor. Doctoral programs frequently require students to enroll in more than one field experience.

Many graduate programs require courses to be taken in a predetermined sequence and won't allow registration for the more advanced courses unless the prerequisite courses have been taken and/or other requirements such as a certain number of years of work or clinical experience, or an appropriate background in research design or statistics, have been met. When looking at the requirements of your program, be sure to carefully review all descriptive materials provided by the program as well as course descriptions in the catalogue to see what, if any, prerequisites are required.

Working with a professor on a one-on-one basis is a form of coursework frequently used in graduate schools. This is called *independent study* or *directed study*. This type of instruction frees the student from regularly scheduled class meetings throughout the semester. The purpose of an independent study class is to allow for the pursuit of individual interests or specializations under the direct supervision or guidance of a particular professor. It may also allow for the development of a particular aspect of the specialization that relatively few graduate students may be interested in. Independent study courses are perfect vehicles to help clarify the thesis or dissertation topic.

The advantages of independent study are obvious: Your learning objectives are the sole concern of the learning experience. Time is not wasted listening to lectures about things already known or listening to the professor responding to student requests to clarify a point that is perfectly clear to you. You are the center of attention and your needs are immediately attended to.

There are downsides to this seemingly utopian situation. Given the opportunity to pursue individual interests at your own schedule may create an obsession with the subject. Hours upon hours may be spent in the library tracking down a very obscure point or bit of knowledge. Although this may be intellectually rewarding, don't lose perspective and waste your time going after an obscure point when that time might have been better spent completing other requirements of the program of study.

Ron, a graduate student in the second to the last semester of a Ph.D. program with a specialization in adult education, provides a good illustration of how a practicum can produce very positive results. Ron was particularly interested in applying the various theories he had learned about adult development in a real situation. He negotiated with his major adviser and arranged to complete a practicum as a curriculum developer in a local adult learning center. It did not take Ron long to realize that the models in use for developing curricula were based on research with youths and children. Little thought or attention had been given to the concept that the center was educating adults, not tall, grown-up children. Ron discussed this with both his major adviser and the administrators of the center and agreed to develop, field-test, and evaluate a new model based on principles of adult development. From Ron's point of view, this was an ideal experience in that he was able to apply his theoretical knowledge in a real setting and the center was able to benefit from his expertise.

The practicum was the most meaningful part of Ron's graduate experience from another perspective as well. Not only was he able to develop, field-test, and evaluate his model, but upon completion of his degree, he was hired as the curriculum developer at the center!

In some graduate schools, there are no predetermined courses whatever. The student consults with his or her adviser and determines the courses to be taken. These types of programs are very good for highly self-directed learners, those with a rich experiential background, or those who have a very good idea not only of what they want to learn but also of how they want to learn it. A clear sense of purpose and objectives as well as good negotiating skills are very helpful in this type of program. Learners need to fully discuss and be particularly adept at negotiating objectives with their committee or chairperson. They also need to be aware of personal reasons for being in the program, and how the suggested courses or other learning experiences will accomplish personal objectives.

Electives are another part of most graduate programs of study. These courses are not required but are available to supplement individual needs or interests in particular fields. They usually provide a greater depth of understanding about the specialization and serve to round out the program of study. They should be selected with the advice of the committee chair or a member of the committee.

It is not uncommon for a graduate program to have student advisers available to help with routine matters. Sometimes student advisers are graduate students themselves and are a very good source of information about departmental courses, concentrations, specializations, and faculty members. They are usually in touch with other students and are part of "the network" or "grapevine" that thrives in most graduate schools.

A word of caution is needed here: Sometimes the student adviser can be perceived as having more authority or knowledge than he or she really has. Remember that, no matter how knowledgeable or well intentioned, a fellow student is not your chair and does not have the authority to make decisions regarding the program of study.

Developing
the Program of Study

Every graduate school has its own way of developing and processing the program of study. This is something that is explained in the program of study material provided by your department or college. Some provide a packet of very formal written documents with all sorts of examples while others provide a list of dates and some blank forms that are refined or developed as needed. As with every bit of paperwork connected with the degree, it is very important to know exactly what forms need to be filled out, when they are due, and who needs to approve them.

In almost every case, the program of study needs to be approved and signed by various college administrators or department faculty. These people may be the members of the graduate committee, the department head, or representatives from the graduate college. It makes good sense to make an appointment and hand carry your program of study forms to each of these people for their signatures. Why? This provides another opportunity to meet with them and discuss how your goals and objectives relate to your program of study. It also gives them an opportunity to get to know you. The importance of getting to know your committee and getting to be known by them can't be stressed enough. This is discussed further in Chapters 3 and 4.

Along with knowing what forms need to be filled out and who needs to approve the program of study, consider how your goals and objectives can be met through the program of study. Questions such as the following will help clarify personal goals and objectives: "Why do I want this degree?" "How will it help me?" "Do I need more courses rather than another degree?" "Am I prepared to invest the necessary time, energy, and resources to get this degree?"

Let's assume that you want a graduate degree for personal reasons and also want to become certified (or licensed) within your profession. This is a common goal of many individuals seeking to earn a graduate degree. It is up to you to know the specific courses or other requirements of the certifying or licensing agency. This information is available through the state, county, or local office charged with this responsibility. In some cases, the professional organizations can provide it. It is important to remember that, although the program of study may be sufficient for the grad college to recommend you for certification or to sit for the licensing exam, the certificate or license is usually granted by the appropriate agency, not the grad college.

Almost every certifying or licensing agency has unique or specific requirements that must be met. Some may require documentation of a certain number of clock hours related to specific profession-related tasks or learning activities. Others may require certain courses with exact prefixes or workshops from a specific professional organization. Still others may require noncredit courses or continuing education units (CEUs) from accredited colleges or universities. Not only is it up to you to know the certification or licensing requirements, it is also to your advantage to think about how these requirements can be met through your program of study.

Keep personal goals and objectives clearly in mind as the program of study is developed. Ask yourself how each course or learning experience will help accomplish your goals.

Try to develop the initial draft of the program of study as much as possible without the assistance of your chair or faculty adviser.

Although this may seem foolish and time wasting, it forces you to become very familiar with the various forms and policies governing the program of study. Often new faculty members are not fully aware of the process and may give incomplete advice. The more experienced faculty members are less apt to give inaccurate or incorrect advice but, let's face it, they will generally give advice that reflects their style or their inclinations. They probably don't know you and your needs as well as you do. Perhaps a person is fairly set in his or her ways and doesn't look for options. This person, although well meaning, might not think about or consider alternatives. Having studied the program of study forms and the department and college policies and procedures, you understand how the system works. This provides you with a stronger rationale when seeking exceptions. The worst that can happen is that the request will be denied.

With an initial draft of the program of study developed as fully as possible, make an appointment to see your committee chair. Use this draft as the basis of discussion. Seek to discuss what you want to do rather than only seeking the chair's ideas about what you should do. All too often, graduate students fall into the traditional student-teacher role and give away their options by asking the adviser such questions as these: "What courses should I take?" "What electives should I take?" "Who should I have on my committee?" You are in a much stronger position when you have thought about these types of questions, discussed them with others, and developed some tentative answers.

A stronger set of questions, and ones that put you on a more equal footing with your adviser, would be the following: "I want to take these courses as they are not only core courses but they also fit into my personal plans. What do you think?" or "I think these electives are appropriate to my objectives and would like your advice on them. What's your opinion?" What you don't want to happen is to be in a position of not having thought about the types of responses you want and then accepting responses that may not be the best ones in your specific situation.

Having a draft in hand and having thought about the concerns as well as the solutions can enable you to better use the meeting to negotiate a program that more accurately reflects your needs and objectives. Tactfully handled, this type of negotiation can positively affect your committee chair and committee members in that it demonstrates that you not only have carefully thought about your reasons for being in graduate school but also have considered ways in which the program of study can facilitate your needs. This can psychologically change committee members' perception of you from the "traditional" student (one who comes to the teacher as a child comes to a parent) to that of a "mature" student (a confident individual seeking the advice of a peer).

Using this approach, students are more able to solicit advice based on specific needs and negotiate a program of study more fully reflecting these goals and objectives rather than getting the cookbook responses often given by faculty.

Once you have met with your chair, have secured the additional needed information, and have negotiated responses acceptable to both, the next step is to revise the draft of the program of study and have it reviewed once again by your committee chair. All that remains is for the other committee members and the department chair of the school to approve it.

Remember that the most important part of the process in developing the program of study is to carefully study the policies and procedures relating to the development of the program of study. Look for ways to accomplish your objectives. This makes developing the program, seeking advice, and negotiating a program that is responsive to your particular concerns much easier.

Sample Program of Study Form

The following is a generic form that can be used to develop your initial draft of your program of study. It is suggested that you use this form or one supplied by your graduate program to complete a sample program. This should not be attempted until after relevant college and departmental policies and procedures have been reviewed and faculty, staff, and fellow students have been consulted.

SAMPLE PROGRAM OF STUDY FORM

	Semester Planned	Semester Completed
CORE COURSES:		

List all core courses here:

SPECIALIZATION OR
 MAJOR COURSES:
List all specialization or major courses here:

ELECTIVES:
List all elective courses here:

INDEPENDENT STUDY:
List all independent study courses here:

Comprehensive Examination:

Proposal Developed:

Proposal Approved:

First Draft of Thesis/
 Dissertation Completed:

Thesis/Dissertation Accepted:

Thesis/Dissertation Defended:

Recognize that the development of the program of study is a series of iterations in that, once the initial draft has been developed, it will probably be revised several times following consultation with others involved in the graduate process.

The completed program of study form should be considered a flexible rather than static document. It will change as a result of courses being added to the schedule that were not available when the program of study was initially developed. It might also be revised due to changes in the schedule that prevent the course from being offered at the time you originally wanted to take it. Perhaps you might want to extend the practicum or internship from one semester to two. It should serve as a guide for planning how to meet academic and professional goals.

Completing Coursework

Completing the courses on the program of study involves advance planning to schedule the courses to fit in with your schedule. It also means going to class, taking notes, preparing for exams, completing required term papers, as well as other class requirements. More important, it means mastering course content.

A conscientious graduate student needs to understand how the courses fit in with personal reasons for being in grad school. How do they relate to areas of research interest? What concerns have piqued curiosity sufficiently to be considered as possible research topics for the dissertation or independent study?

The proposal, thesis/dissertation, and the oral defense are also considered part of the program of study. These are discussed more fully in Chapters 5 and 6. Ideally, these culminating experiences evolve from the completion of the coursework listed in the program of study. The connections between the courses and literature being reviewed for course term papers and the thesis/dissertation are logical and easy to see. When the connections have been made, the graduate student makes an easy transition from taking courses to writing the final product.

If grades are important, be attuned to the subtleties of the classroom and seek to understand the little things that are important to the professor in addition to the course objectives and requirements presented in the syllabus. It is quite possible to determine if the professor values discussion by the way in which questions or requests for elaboration are handled. If this seems to be valued, it makes sense to ask meaningful questions and thoughtful requests for elaboration. If it is not seemingly valued, the astute graduate student will keep quiet and find other ways to get answers to questions and not jeopardize the grade by unwittingly antagonizing the professor.

Time Management

To complete the program, you need to be able to manage your time. As discussed in Chapter 1, it is very difficult to add the demands of a graduate degree to the many demands already placed on your time. It probably isn't possible to continue to do everything you have always done in addition to completing your degree. Something has to go in order for you to maintain your sanity and keep in control of your life. More than likely you won't fully realize all that is required until the process begins. A usual reaction is to think: "I have bitten off more than I can chew" or "I wish there were more hours in the day."

Good time management begins with a clarification and prioritization of personal objectives. To gain some control over your time, it is a good idea to make time management a part of your everyday routine. How much time is needed and how much time can realistically be spent *every day* on such tasks as reading, thinking, writing, doing research at the library, and other similarly related degree tasks? Schedule time every day for these activities and keep to the schedule. Resist the temptation to take a long, hot bath during the time set aside to write or study.

At the end of each day, pause and reflect on those things that were scheduled to be done. Were they done? Yes? No? Why not? How can today's errors not be repeated tomorrow? Only you can effectively plan your time and only you can accept the blame or receive the credit concerning the accomplishment of daily objectives. Set realistic goals and plan your time wisely and effectively!

Time Wasters

One of the most useful things to do when trying to maintain control of your life is to think of those things that waste time and then do something to get rid of the time wasters. The following is a list of the time wasters that apply to most graduate students:

1. Telephone interruptions
2. Friends or relatives dropping in uninvited when you are studying
3. Lack of clarity regarding learning objectives, priorities, and deadlines
4. Indecision and procrastination
5. Poor time management
6. Fatigue
7. Crisis management
8. Inability to say "no"

Take a good hard look at this list. How many of the time wasters apply to you? Do you let the telephone interrupt your working time? Why? Why not let it ring? Don't answer it; let the answering machine take the call. If you don't have an answering machine, get one. It is well worth the cost in terms of time management. This way you can complete the term paper during the time set aside to do it rather than letting someone else control your time. How about item 3 (lack of clarity regarding learning objectives, priorities, and deadlines)? How often have you set an objective and really stuck to the deadline you gave yourself to complete it? Item 8 (inability to say "no") is another problem for many people. Think about this—just because someone asks you to do something is no reason that you have to agree to it. Feel free to say "no" and don't feel guilty. Don't even feel the need to give an explanation. You are completing your degree and that is most important.

Know Yourself

You are one of your most important resources. You consist of a mind, a body, and a spirit. There is much to be said regarding the interconnectedness of the mind, body, and spirit and their relationship to completing a graduate degree.

The Mind

There are very little hard data about how the mind functions. We are sure, however, that each person's mind is unique and each of us learns in a variety of ways. Some learn best from a lecture. Others prefer reading. Still others prefer to interact with material and contemplate the implications on a personal level. This notion is not new. The ancient Hindus viewed the different learning styles of people as active, passive, emotional, and thoughtful. The *Bhagavad Gita*, one of the holy books of the Hindus, suggested that these four learning elements were the four basic yogas, or pathways, needed to practice religion.

In the past century, many psychologists and learning theorists have proposed a variety of theories to describe learning styles and how the mind processes learning. There is no agreement on this. Researchers are still trying to agree on an acceptable definition of learning and the psychological, emotional, and volitional factors that affect learning.

The Body

Keeping in good physical shape is another way of ensuring completion of the graduate program. Most graduate students only think about the "mental" requirements when contemplating their degree. The "physical" side of the equation is equally important as well.

When reading textbooks or reviewing class notes in preparation for an exam, it is not uncommon to spend several hours in basically one position. This is hard on the body because blood circulation is restricted and muscles tend to tighten up. It also contributes to a feeling of being tired, which is a frequent lament of graduate learners.

The more sedentary one is, the less opportunity for adequate blood flow. Blood carries oxygen to all parts of the body. Without an adequate oxygen supply, there is a tendency to feel tired and listless. An easy solution is to make it a point to get up and walk around several times while studying. This allows for better circulation and may help avoid cramping and that tired feeling that often accompanies studying.

Another good way to recoup the energy lost while studying is to do something physical on a regular basis. Jogging or walking every day helps to keep the body in shape and helps keep the energy level up. Joggers who also happen to be graduate students frequently use running time as "think" time and have found a good way to condition their body while using their mind. Many students find that a carefully planned exercise regimen at a local health and fitness club does wonders for maintaining the energy level required to complete a graduate program.

Playing racquetball or taking an aerobics or exercise class is another way of keeping in shape. These types of programs exercise the heart and lungs and assist these organs to better perform their vital functions. Any program designed to increase blood flow and oxygenation will result in greater energy levels.

Good nutrition is important to completing a graduate program. There is ample evidence to suggest that good nutrition leads to healthier and longer lives. Good nutrition also increases powers of concentration. Although donuts and coffee might keep you awake and provide a temporary energy boost, they are not as effective in the long run as proper nutrition. A commercially prepared energy supplement low in calories and high in vitamins and nutrients does a more effective job in restoring needed energy.

As with any physical fitness or nutritional program, it is advisable to consult with a physician, dietitian, nutritionist, or other appropriate specialist to determine the best program.

The Spirit

The definition of *spirit* is up to you. Some may define it as "the soul" and seek to develop it through meditation or religious activity.

Others may define it as one's unique essence. What is being suggested here is that, regardless of how it is defined, it is important not to neglect it when completing the graduate program.

If you believe spirit is defined through a particular religious preference, don't forget about religion while engrossed in graduate studies. Stay true to your beliefs. There are many individuals who are firm in the belief that prayers do not go unanswered. If this is part of your religious belief system, don't let the stress of completing your program of study obscure the power of prayer. Use prayer if it will help relieve the stress and strain of graduate studies.

No discussion of the spirit would be complete without a word about keeping spirits up. It is important to remember that a graduate degree should be perceived as a means to an end, not the end itself. Many graduate students put too much stress on themselves by thinking that the world will end if they don't get the degree. Perhaps the only sure thing that can be said in this book is that, as of today, many graduate students have not gotten their degrees and, in spite of all the doomsday prophecies, the world has not ended.

Although it is important to recognize and acknowledge that a great deal of time, energy, and money is being invested in completing the degree, it is equally important to recognize that, no matter how difficult it may be, life will go on even if you do not complete the degree. Lighten up and have fun.

Controlling Frustrations

Life as a graduate student can be a frustrating process. It is filled with very high "highs" and very low "lows." Graduate students constantly face uncertainties commonly associated with almost every graduate program that ever existed. In many ways, it is an emotional roller coaster.

The "highs" are times of absolute euphoria, like "acing" a test, completing a truly wonderful term paper that draws the praise of your professor, passing the comps, having your proposal finally accepted, completing the thesis or dissertation, or, best of all, graduating. These are the times when you see the light at the end of the tunnel and feel that the struggles are all worth it.

The "lows" are the times when you hate your faculty adviser, committee chair, committee members, the dean, the department chair, the professors, and everything and everyone remotely associated with your program. These times come when you are faced with situations over which you can exert little or no control, such as not knowing what to study for the final exam or what will be on the comprehensive exam, or having to sit through a terribly boring course with an instructor who rambles on forever. Equally frustrating times come when trying to get your committee to sign off on your proposal or trying to convince the department chair that the course taken before you transferred is the same one he now says needs to be retaken because it has a different prefix. These are the times you really want to scream, kick the dog, and yell at everyone!

There is also the general stress associated just with being a graduate student and being treated like a number rather than a person. Long lines at registration, computer breakdowns, not knowing what will happen after graduation, and wondering how to get the money for next semester's tuition are common in the life of a graduate student.

A frequent frustration of graduate students relates to faculty members returning the thesis or dissertation for revisions and seemingly being either unaware or unconcerned about the emotional distress this is creating. When this is discussed with the professor, a common response is that the revisions are needed to make the document as good as it can be. "After all," the faculty member says, "I have been through this many times before and I know what is needed to make this academically acceptable. Trust me." How can you argue with this? After all, the professor does have expertise and experience in this sort of thing. You do not. Even so, it is a frustrating experience and one that almost every graduate student will encounter.

A good bit of advice when you are experiencing frustration associated with a particular issue is to allow some time to pass before dealing with the issue. The passage of time helps reduce frustration.

As the author of this book, I can relate to frustration. After a contract to publish this book was signed, my editor made several suggestions for improving the manuscript. I made them and sent in the revised manuscript thinking that I was done with revisions. Not so! In fact, the book you are now reading has been substantially revised many times after the contract to publish was signed. Each time, my initial reaction was to think: "Oh, come on! Not again! It's fine the way it is! It doesn't need any further revisions. After all, I know what I'm talking about." I was frustrated.

However, following my own advice, I let some time pass before responding to the suggestions. This distanced me from my frustration and helped me realize that most of the suggestions really did improve the book. I was able to negotiate the changes once I had dealt with my frustrations.

It needs to be stressed that it is perfectly normal for the lives of graduate students to be filled with many frustrations and upheavals. More important is finding ways to control them.

"RID": HOW TO CONTROL FRUSTRATION

1. *R*ecognize that you are frustrated.
2. *I*dentify the source of your frustration.
3. *D*eal realistically with the frustration.

The first step in dealing with frustration is to *recognize* you are experiencing frustration and admit it to yourself. Although this may sound very basic, it is not always easy to recognize and admit that you are frustrated. It is, however, key to do so. Many of us are pretty good at covering up our emotions, especially if we feel that to be emotional or frustrated is socially unacceptable or if we were conditioned to feel that adults shouldn't show their emotions. Thus an important first step in controlling frustration is to admit being frustrated.

Once frustration is recognized, the next step is to carefully *identify* the true source of the frustration. This also is not as easy as it seems because sometimes the source of the frustration is oneself and this can be hard to accept. For example, have you ever blamed the noise the children were making when you were studying for your not doing well on a test when the real reason was that you simply didn't prepare sufficiently? Psychologists tell us that we frequently blame others for our shortcomings rather than accept the blame ourselves. Blaming others helps maintain self-esteem. To deal with frustration, the real source must be identified. Are you frustrated with your professor for making you revise the document or are you frustrated with yourself because you don't want to do any more revising?

The final step is to *deal* realistically with the frustration. As mentioned earlier, a good approach is to let some time pass before confronting the source of frustration. During this time, develop a realistic plan of action for dealing with the frustration. Only you can decide what is realistic and reasonable as only you can judge if it will work given your knowledge of the situation.

As a general rule, if the source of frustration is another person, increased communication will probably help. If the source is yourself, you may need to find a way to release the frustration. Physical exercise, reading for pleasure, engaging in a hobby, or finding some other way to dissipate the pent-up frustration will help because frustration, like any form of energy, will not go away and needs to be released.

Financial Aid Publications

Complete College Financing Guide (2nd ed.). Barron's Educational Series, Inc., 250 Wireless Boulevard, Hauppauge, NY 11788.

Fellowships and Grants. American Council of Learned Societies, 228 E. 45th Street, New York, NY 10017-3398.

Fellowships: United States of America and Canada. John Simon Guggenheim Memorial Foundation, 90 Park Avenue, New York, NY 10026.

Financial Aid for Graduate and Professional Education. Peterson's, P.O. Box 2133, Princeton, NJ 08543-2123.

Fulbright and Other Grants for Graduate Study Abroad. Institute of International Education, 809 United Nations Plaza, New York, NY 10027.

The Graduate Scholarship Book: The Complete Guide to Scholarships, Fellowships, Grants, and Loans for Graduate and Professional Study. Prentice Hall, 200 Old Tappan Road, Old Tappan, NJ 07675.

Graduate Study and You: A Guide for Prospective Graduate Students. Council of Graduate Schools, One Dupont Circle, N.W., Suite 430, Washington, DC 20036.

Grant Guidelines. New York Council for the Humanities, 33 West 42nd Street, New York, NY 10036.

The Grants Register. St. Martin's Press, 175 Fifth Avenue, New York, NY 10010.

Overview of Endowment Programs. National Endowment for the Humanities, 1100 Pennsylvania Avenue, N.W., Washington, DC 20506.

THREE

The Graduate Committee

Considering graduate school was difficult. I am a professor in a local college and I'm used to being in charge of my program. How could I let the professors at the "U" know that I didn't know everything and still keep my self-respect? Would I pick the right program? The right committee?

Talking with colleagues, administrators, friends, and other students gave me some ideas about what might work for me. My doubts were reduced to workable challenges and I was able to benefit greatly.

Bill

Perhaps the most important people in your entire graduate program are those who form your graduate committee. Collectively and individually, these individuals have a great deal of power related to the completion of your degree. Frequently, the committee will approve everything from the initial draft of the program of study through the final copy of the thesis or dissertation. Because they have real influence on your future, it is important to learn about the functions of the committee, its relation to the program of study, the different roles the various committee members play, and how to select an effective committee.

Functions of the Graduate Committee

Depending on the college or university, there are various functions of the graduate committee. In some instances, the committee as a whole is intimately involved with every aspect of the graduate program. In other cases, the committee may serve as a "rubber stamp" for the committee chair in that the chair makes most decisions and the committee does little other than approve them.

Most graduate committees perform one or more of the functions shown in the following list:

1. Approve the program of study
2. Develop and respond to the comprehensive examination
3. Approve the idea (or proposal) for the thesis or dissertation
4. Accept the final copy of the thesis or dissertation
5. Respond to the oral defense or presentation of the thesis or dissertation

The Program of Study

In Chapter 2, we discussed how to develop and complete the program of study. What is the role of the graduate committee in all of this?

In most universities, the graduate committee members can provide advice and direction beyond their official responsibilities and that which is readily available through routine printed matter such as graduate college catalogues or departmental guides. Realistically, members of graduate committees have been at the university longer than you have and can provide "behind-the-scenes" understandings of what can be done and what can't be done, what rules can be bent and what regulations are inflexible. They are more aware of the subtleties of the committee process and usually are more willing to maneuver and manipulate the process to accomplish their objectives, your objectives, and the objectives of the graduate program. These are the types of professors you want on your committee because they know how the system works and will make it work for you.

They are important people to know for other professional reasons. Let's assume that Professor Barbara Smith is your committee chair and that the other members of your committee have been selected. More is said about how to select committee members later in this chapter (see the section "Choosing Your Committee"). You have presented yourself well, are perceived as being competent, and seem to have a good rapport with committee members. In this situation, it is quite common for your chair and other committee members to take a professional interest in your success as a graduate student and as a professional in the field.

This manifests itself in a number of ways. For example, Professor Smith comes to know you and your abilities. She recognizes your potential. You appreciate her reputation and influence in the field. A natural outgrowth is that she becomes your mentor and begins a mentoring relationship that may last far beyond graduation.

In many universities, grants are written by professors as one means of furthering their research and service agendas. If the relationship with your chair or other committee members is solid, it is logical that they would view you as a research assistant on one of their grants or would be willing to help you write a grant of your own.

Perhaps one of the most important manifestations of a good relationship comes when looking for a job. This is when committee members and other faculty can help, particularly if they are well connected and respected in their fields. It is amazing how many graduates find a new position or are promoted as a direct result of action by a professor.

What is not so obvious is that some professors know how the system works better than others. Those who are less adept at this often are less willing to do anything other than to perform routine committee functions in the traditional, time-honored manner. These individuals usually don't allow you much room to maneuver. They tend to operate in a rather predictable and pedantic manner. Although they won't work against you, they won't particularly work for you either.

It doesn't take much more than reading the provided department materials and talking with veteran students to know what the full committee needs to approve and what they don't. When signatures are required as proof of approval, be certain to obtain them yourself. Don't rely on other committee members to get them. They are busy and, even with the best intentions, they may not get it done. After all, it's your program. You need to be certain that everything that needs to be done is done. Don't take a chance and leave it to someone else, no matter how willing he or she is to take this on.

If each committee member needs to sign off to indicate approval of the program of study, use this as a time to meet with this person to discuss and negotiate your program of study. Discuss any unusual, different, or extraordinary courses, practica, internships, field experiences, or other learning experiences.

Comprehensive Examination

Quite often the members of the graduate committee are responsible for preparing and responding to (grading) your comprehensive examination (a.k.a. comps). In Chapter 4, we will discuss the exam in detail. But for now, it is sufficient to say that the comps consist of a written and/or an oral component and are designed to demonstrate competency regarding the program of study. The comprehensive exam frequently serves as a "rite of passage" in that, once it is successfully completed, the student is usually admitted to candidacy and can begin work on the thesis or dissertation.

Often graduate schools ask that committee members supply the questions for the comprehensive exam. In this situation, it is very important that members of your committee know you and your strengths and weaknesses. Taking this into account, it is a good idea to make an appointment to meet individually with committee members and to seek their advice about the content of the exam. Be direct regarding your concerns, yet also be tactful. The worst thing that can happen when asking for advice about the questions on the comp is to be told nothing. Even in this worst-case scenario you still have gained something as you have created another opportunity to interact and negotiate with your committee.

Many committee members recognize that it is virtually impossible to prepare for everything that might appear on a comp. In this spirit, it is not uncommon to receive fairly direct and succinct responses when asking what to study and how to prepare for the exam. For example, in meeting with committee member X, you might be lucky and be given the areas of concern that this professor usually develops into comp questions. In the meeting with Professor Smith, it might be learned that she feels class exams are her way of emphasizing major concepts or strategies. This is an extremely valuable bit of information as she virtually has told you what to review. In these best-case scenarios, you not only have met with your committee members but also have saved a lot of time and unnecessary worry.

Committee members usually have the task of determining the form and content of the oral exam as well as the written one. They may use the oral to ask for elaboration or clarification of a response on the written part. In some graduate programs, the oral is a time when a completely different set of questions are asked because committee members may want to see how the student processes the question before responding or how well he or she thinks under pressure.

On one occasion, a very bright and very verbal doctoral student (let's call him Joe) was taking his oral comprehensive exam in anthropology. It was scheduled to be from 1:00 to 2:30 p.m. Three of the four committee members had another exam later that afternoon. Joe knew he had done well on the written comp and was expecting few problems on the oral.

Joe was quick to respond and gave long, obtuse responses when brief, direct answers were called for. Joe thought he was in control and doing a great job of limiting the questions with his long and involved responses. What he didn't realize was that the committee members were becoming angry with him for wasting valuable time. About an hour into the exam, the committee chair stood up and dramatically interrupted one of Joe's long-winded responses by announcing that the committee had a series of questions that needed to be asked and that they would be asked and answered now! Furthermore, he said the exam would end in 30 minutes and that if Joe did not respond to each and every question, he would probably fail the exam. Joe had totally misread the committee. Fortunately, he was able to recover and made the rest of his answers more concise. The committee members were able to ask their questions in the remaining time, and he successfully passed the exam. Joe almost failed because he did not clearly understanding the requirements of the comp. He should have discussed this more carefully with his committee chair.

At many colleges, another function of graduate committees is to evaluate or grade the exam. Committee members have several options related to this task.

It is best for you when the committee members are unanimous in their decision to pass you on your comps. This signals full support and recognition of the successful completion of the preliminary phase of the program of study, and tacit approval to begin work on the thesis or dissertation.

The committee may decide on a "provisional" pass. This means they have concerns with the exam and will usually describe what needs to be done to successfully complete the exam. If this happens, it is very important to check with each committee member for additional information about what went wrong and the specific concerns of each committee member. This calls for a series of careful, tactful, and well-planned meetings with each committee member.

The worst result is a vote of failure on the comp. Although this is not a frequent occurrence, it does happen. If it happens to you, it is imperative to talk with your committee chair, your department head, and/or the graduate college to determine your options.

The Proposal, Thesis, and/or Dissertation

In Chapter 5, information about the proposal, the thesis, and the dissertation is presented. Committee members also provide advice and assistance regarding the development of these parts of the graduate program of study. They usually enjoy this function more than evaluating the comp as it is less stressful for all concerned.

Throughout this chapter, the importance of becoming known by your committee members and of them getting to know you, has been stressed. By so doing, you are building a relationship that will continue through the comps, the proposal, and the thesis or dissertation.

The better you and your ideas are known to the committee, the better will be the level of communication and understanding. The more time and effort expended on this, the easier for the committee to understand your intentions and provide relevant, appropriate advice.

Roles of Committee Members

On most graduate committees, there is a chairperson and from one to four other members. Depending on the policy of the graduate program, committee members are usually appointed either by the graduate college or by the department head. Before appointments are made, the administration and proposed faculty consult to ensure an equitable distribution of the departmental workload, compatibility with the student, faculty interest, and content expertise regarding the initial interest(s) of the learner.

You should play an integral part in the selection of committee members. As always, be sure to follow the university or department policies and procedures governing the establishment of the committee. If there are no formal policies, be certain to know when the committee is formed, how it is formed, the number of required members, and the functions of each member. Formalize your suggestions regarding potential committee members by sending recommendations in writing to the administrator or professor who has final responsibility for making committee selections.

In varying degrees, each committee member's roles and responsibilities are shown in the following list:

1. To advise you regarding course selection, program development and completion, the comprehensive exam, the proposal, and the thesis or dissertation
2. To direct your work regarding independent study, the practicum, and/or the internship
3. To supervise your work as a teaching or research assistant
4. To provide assistance regarding job prospects

Chairperson or Major Adviser

Probably the most important person in your graduate school life is the *chairperson* or *major adviser* of your committee. There is no single job description that adequately defines this role. Clearly such things as the prevailing policy of the department or college and the temperament, style, experience, research expertise, and concern of the individual all come into play when discussing this function. As mentioned earlier, this person may serve as a mentor and may be quite influential in helping you secure financial aid and in finding a job after graduation.

In almost every university, faculty members exercise a great deal of autonomy. How they teach, supervise, chair, coordinate, direct, or facilitate is based on their experience and understanding of their position regardless of what is stated as policy. The same holds true regarding their roles as committee members and committee chairs. Whether this is right or wrong is not the issue. It is frequently a fact of graduate college life and one you have to understand and live with.

Few, if any, committee chairs have ever had any formal training or preparation for this role. The prevailing feeling seems to be that having gone through a similar program as a graduate student, having completed a graduate degree, being on graduate committees, or being appointed to the graduate faculty is sufficient preparation for serving as a committee chair. Although this may seem inefficient, this has been going on for years and can be used to your advantage, as is shown later in this chapter (see "Choosing Your Committee," pp. 56-58).

Regardless of the way in which your committee chair functions, you need to do a great deal of listening, discussing, and negotiating during this process. The vast majority of graduate departments have never given thought to educating chairs on how to listen, how to lead, or how to reconcile differences. Most acquire this knowledge by working with students and asking questions of their colleagues. Trial and error serves as a good teacher. Those who take this role seriously become good in a relatively short time. Once their reputations become established, they are sought out as they are known to be helpful, knowledgeable, student oriented, and competent.

There are faculty members who really don't like being on committees. They see this function as taking time from their other university interests such as research and publishing. Others feel that current teaching, research, and service responsibilities leave them little time for advising. They may view advising as too time consuming and resent the intrusion. The grapevine is usually quite active about these faculty but, unfortunately, this does not prevent them from being assigned as a committee chair or member.

Regardless of whether or not your chairperson has a wonderful or a horrible reputation, the chairperson has power and needs to be treated with respect. Realize that, without the cooperation of the committee chair, it will be difficult to complete your program. This does not mean acquiescing to each and every suggestion that is made but it does suggest a need to carefully, skillfully, and tactfully negotiate with your chair. For each suggestion that is made, ask yourself questions such as these: "Is it a valid point?" "How much will it improve my work?" "What additional work will I need to do to incorporate the suggestion?" or "What will I gain or lose if the suggestion is questioned?" The advantages and disadvantages of questioning the advice or suggestion of any committee member, especially the chair, must be given top priority and be very carefully considered.

Other Committee Roles

Of lesser importance are the roles of the other committee members. This is *not* to say that the other committee members are not important. Clearly they are. Just as you would carefully listen to your committee chair, the views, thoughts, and suggestions of the other committee members need to be very carefully considered throughout the process for you to succeed and retain control of your graduate school odyssey.

The roles of committee members lend themselves to the purpose of the committee—to provide advice and assistance regarding the completion of the program of study. To accomplish this, committee members may be assigned to your committee based on their knowledge of process and/or content. This means that a committee member possessing knowledge of the research process may be assigned to your committee to ensure that at least one committee member can provide expert advice regarding research design or methodology. Another member may be assigned based on knowledge of specific content. In this way, at least one committee member has content expertise and can be relied on to provide this assistance as needed.

Committee membership based on differing functions creates a system of checks and balances and may help avoid a committee being dominated by the committee chair or a particularly strong-willed member. Soliciting advice and opinions from all committee members also may help avoid dominance by one member as this helps to ensure that all committee members have a stake in the process. It also may provide different opinions regarding appropriate research design, course selection, or other program variables.

As part of the checks and balances system, many graduate school deans assign a dean's representative to the committee. This person usually provides little in terms of process and content advice and mainly is assigned to ensure that quality control standards of the college or university are adhered to strictly and impartially.

Getting to Know
Potential Committee Members

It makes very good sense to know your committee because, regardless of why they have been appointed or whether they have developed the comprehensive exam questions, they have a major impact on the outcome of the exam.

The easiest way to do this is by enrolling in the course(s) of department professors who may become a member of your committee. If the course(s) are part of the program of study, this not only fulfills a program requirement but also provides an opportunity to observe this person at work. During the term or semester, personal concerns, areas of expertise, research interests, peeves, pet projects, and topics of interest will be mentioned. Be sure to note these when they are identified.

Noting these concerns is a good idea even if the person does not become a committee member as it can result in a better understanding of the goals and objectives of the course. It also is a good way of gaining insights into those things that are important to the instructor. Knowing this may result in a better grade.

While in the course, try to get a feel for this person as a committee member. How well do you think he or she would respond to your ideas or interact with the other potential members of your committee? How do you feel about this person as a possible committee chair?

Becoming Known by Potential Committee Members

Being in a course offered by a potential committee member is a two-way street because it gives the professor an opportunity to get to know you as well. It is important to make a good impression. Give thoughtful answers to questions posed in class, make an extra effort to ensure that all class assignments are done in a timely manner and at a graduate level. Definitely don't be late for class. If anything, try to arrive a few minutes early. Whatever you do, don't doze off!

Try to find legitimate reasons to meet with the instructor. One-to-one meetings allow the professor to get to know you as more than a member of the class. Your strengths, your personality, your individuality become known.

For example, the ability to compare, contrast, analyze, synthesize, and integrate information is a goal of most graduate education (see the section in Chapter 4, "Compare, Contrast, Analyze, Synthesize, and Integrate"). This is often what differentiates graduate from undergraduate school. You are well advised to use class discussion to develop and practice this skill.

Let's say that you are in a seminar in which there is ample time for discussion. Used wisely, this is a great opportunity to demonstrate your ability to compare and contrast what is being presented with other relevant information, theories, or theorists known to the field. Also use term papers, class presentations, or essay exams to demonstrate your ability to synthesize what has been written or discussed to develop a new idea or application. These are the types of behaviors and responses that most graduate faculty are looking for. Once they realize you are capable of this type of response, they are more likely to view you as a competent professional and one on whose committee they might like to serve.

Make yourself known within your department by volunteering to serve as a student representative if and when the opportunity presents itself. Meet with the graduate dean, department chair, or various faculty to discuss aspects of the graduate program that you particularly like or feel may need clarification. If a staff member has been helpful to you, write a letter (with copies to appropriate supervisory personnel) thanking that person. When this type of assertive behavior is handled well, it goes a long way toward helping you become known as a real person rather than a number or simply "another graduate student." It can also help to ensure that your suggestions and comments relating to your graduate committee may be listened to as well.

When trying to become better known by your committee, be careful not to push too hard. Keep in mind that faculty have many responsibilities other than serving as a committee member. They are involved in their own research, teaching, and service activities and serve as committee members to many other learners.

The key to becoming known by your committee members is the careful, skillful, and tactful way in which you do it. Don't be too obvious. Keep in mind that faculty may recognize and resent being manipulated. Be mindful and respectful of their time. They have other obligations and value their time. Don't waste it.

Choosing Your Committee

It is vital to know the process by which committee members are selected or assigned. Speak with fellow students, graduates, and faculty to get this information. Be certain to obtain any and all brochures, handouts, or other material describing policy or procedures relative to committee selection and/or appointment. Once you have this information, read it carefully. Seldom, if ever, are students specifically prohibited from suggesting specific committee members. In fact, many administrators welcome student input because it can make the committee selection process smoother and more efficient.

A well-functioning committee is very important to the successful completion of your graduate program. It makes sense to take an assertive role in all aspects of committee selection. A key way to retain some control over this part of the program is to carefully consider those faculty with whom you work well or those faculty with whom you have developed a good feeling about as a result of having been in their course. Feel free to suggest that they be assigned or appointed to serve on your committee.

There is no "best" way to choose a committee. Each graduate college or department has its own policies and procedures for doing so. In some programs, the process is rather formal. Policy guides are provided, manuals are to be closely followed, checklists need to be checked off, forms need to be filled out, and rigid due dates are set for everything. Other programs operate in such a loose manner that it is a wonder that committees are ever formed! Still other programs combine form and process with creativity and encourage individuals to develop innovative programs that truly reflect individual needs and objectives.

Regardless of the type of graduate program you are in, it is very important to consider the qualities you are looking for in committee members. Don't be afraid to ask questions and to negotiate concerns with faculty. Don't operate on hearsay, rumors, or innuendo. Don't be persuaded by the advice of other students regardless of how well intentioned they might be. Check it out for yourself. Do everything you need to do to really understand the process.

Become involved with the process at every level. Don't wait for things to happen. Take the initiative and make them happen. This might mean writing letters suggesting potential committee members or meeting with your adviser, department head, or graduate dean to offer suggestions. Do whatever is necessary to get a committee that works well with one another, understands your learning style, and, perhaps most important, will work for your success.

Committee Member Selection Guide

The following question is frequently raised by graduate students when seeking committee members: "How do I know what to look for in a potential committee member?" The Committee Member Selection Guide (CMSG) has been designed to help you determine which characteristics of effective committee members are important to you and the degree to which faculty demonstrate attainment of those characteristics.

The CMSG is a list of characteristics of effective graduate committee members as perceived by graduate students I have worked with over a 20-year period. This is not a definitive list and no claims are made regarding its reliability or validity. It is included as an aid in collecting and evaluating information about faculty who might serve as members of your graduate committee.

Copy the CMSG from the end of this chapter and complete one for each faculty member you are even remotely considering for your committee.

Committee Member
Selection ʻGuide (CMSG)

Directions: (a) In the blank *before* each characteristic of effective committee members, place an *"I"* if you feel this characteristic is *important* to you OR place an *"N"* if you feel it is *not* important to you. (b) Use the following rating scale for the second part of this activity.

0	1	2	3	4	5

0 = Absent OR unable to determine
1 = Low attainment
3 = Moderate attainment
5 = High attainment

For those characteristics you have rated as "important," place a check mark (✓) above the appropriate number to indicate your perception of the degree to which the potential committee member has demonstrated attainment of that characteristic.

POTENTIAL COMMITTEE MEMBER _____
(Name)

____ 1. Shows fairness

0	1	2	3	4	5

____ 2. Has a sense of humor

0	1	2	3	4	5

____ 3. Has subject matter expertise

0	1	2	3	4	5

____ 4. Shares my interests

0	1	2	3	4	5

____ 5. Is a good communicator

0	1	2	3	4	5

____ 6. Is a good negotiator

0	1	2	3	4	5

____ 7. Asks probing questions

0	1	2	3	4	5

____ 8. Knows the literature of the field

0	1	2	3	4	5

____ 9. Is professional in relationships

0	1	2	3	4	5

____10. Relates well to graduate students

0	1	2	3	4	5

____11. Considers individual differences

0	1	2	3	4	5

____12. Suggests ways in which information may be applied

0	1	2	3	4	5

____13. Is well prepared

0	1	2	3	4	5

____14. Motivates interest in learning

0	1	2	3	4	5

____15. Is well organized

0	1	2	3	4	5

____16. Is a good listener

| 0 | 1 | 2 | 3 | 4 | 5 |

____17. Is enthusiastic

| 0 | 1 | 2 | 3 | 4 | 5 |

____18. Is flexible

| 0 | 1 | 2 | 3 | 4 | 5 |

____19. Has good research skills

| 0 | 1 | 2 | 3 | 4 | 5 |

____20. Is experienced as a committee member

| 0 | 1 | 2 | 3 | 4 | 5 |

____21. Maintains office hours or is available to meet with students

| 0 | 1 | 2 | 3 | 4 | 5 |

____22. Is open and honest

| 0 | 1 | 2 | 3 | 4 | 5 |

____23. Is structured

| 0 | 1 | 2 | 3 | 4 | 5 |

____24. Is supportive

| 0 | 1 | 2 | 3 | 4 | 5 |

____25. Sets deadlines

| 0 | 1 | 2 | 3 | 4 | 5 |

Discussion: The CMSG provides a profile regarding your perceptions of the degree to which faculty members exhibit characteristics of effective committee members. Characteristics rated 3 or higher are acceptable levels of attainment. Faculty members demonstrating "moderate" to "high" levels of attainment on those characteristics important to you probably would be effective committee members.

FOUR

The Comprehensive Exam

I was scared stiff at the thought of returning to school, taking courses, and having to pass exams. I never did well on written exams and, as a result, had some doubts about my ability to complete a graduate degree. Could I sit in class, take notes, write papers, and study for tests the same way I did when I was an undergrad?

Well, I'm now in grad school and doing quite well. My family and I have discussed my concerns and we all have made the necessary adjustments. I'm preparing for my comps. I know it's only a matter of time before I graduate.

Paulette

Graduate programs frequently have something called a "comprehensive examination." The "comp" usually is taken during the last semester of coursework or immediately after coursework has been completed. It is designed to demonstrate mastery of the program of study.

Many, but not all, master's degree programs have a comp. It is very unusual for doctoral programs not to have one. Comps are most often a written exam lasting anywhere from 2 hours to 2 days. Many schools follow the written exam with an oral exam designed to provide further evidence of mastery of the program of study.

Some have only an oral. For those graduate programs in which the comp is offered, passing it is a major milestone.

Graduate students approach the comp with a feeling of dread and fear. For many, the thought of this type of exam causes the body to ache and the mind to turn to mush. This perception is especially true for the learner who has a bachelor's degree and has been out of school for a number of years and is thinking of returning to graduate school. Having completed an undergraduate degree does little to lessen the dread and fear. However, it is important to recognize that attainment of the bachelor's degree is indicative of success and demonstrates an ability to take exams regardless of how many years ago it was completed.

Purpose of the
Comprehensive Examination

As mentioned, the purpose of the comprehensive exam is to demonstrate to the committee and the graduate college your mastery of the program of study.

In many doctoral programs, the comp determines whether the learner is ready to be admitted to candidacy. Being admitted to candidacy means that the learner has completed coursework, has passed the comp, and is now ready to proceed with proposal development and completion of the dissertation. Students are frequently referred to as being "ABD" (all but dissertation) when they have completed their comps.

The Comprehensive
Examination Process

Comprehensive examinations are usually given at the end of the program of study but before completion of the proposal or thesis or dissertation. They may consist of a written exam, an oral exam, or both. At some institutions, the exams are individualized to reflect unique programs of study, but at others it may be a standardized exam developed by the faculty of the department or program. Regardless of which method is used, the questions seek evidence of competence regarding coursework described in the program of study (i.e., the core, the specialization, research). Most often the committee chair or adviser prepares the exam and makes arrangements to administer and evaluate it.

The Written Comp

When the comp is *individually* developed, the chair prepares questions, obtains additional questions, usually from the committee members, and designs the comp. It is best if the examinee has completed a course or two with the committee members and has an idea of the concepts or ideas that are important to each. As discussed in Chapter 3, committee members usually ask questions reflecting their particular areas of interest and/or expertise. Knowing this gives more of an idea of the nature of the questions that will be asked.

A *standardized* comp means that everyone takes the same exam at the same time on the same day. The standardized comp format attempts to ensure that everyone is treated equally and that no one has an advantage over anyone else. The dates for the exam are usually scheduled well in advance but it clearly is the students' responsibility to know when the exam is scheduled. With standardized comps, the exam is usually drawn from a pool of questions developed over the years. The department head or the dean may appoint a committee charged with developing a new exam each year. Whatever the process, standardized exams are more stressful as it is frequently more difficult to anticipate the questions.

After the written exam has been administered, it is rated, evaluated, or graded by the chair, by the committee members, or by a departmental committee. When the exam is reviewed with no knowledge of whose written exam is being read, it is being read *blind.* The readers do not know whose exam they are reading. When a department uses standardized exams, they are most often read blind.

The Oral Comp

Many graduate programs follow the written part of the comp with an oral part. Some do not. Just as there is no set way of developing or administering the written part, there is no set way of developing or administering the oral part. Nor is there any uniform way to determine the purpose or nature of the oral, the time provided between the written and the oral parts of the exam, or circumstances when the oral may be optional or omitted. Make it your business to know these things. Talk with your committee chair, department head, graduate school counselor, or adviser. If an oral follows the written comp, be sure to know when the oral is administered (one day following the written exam? one week later? two weeks later?) and the circumstances under which it is administered. For example, does the student make these arrangements or does the department secretary or administrative assistant do this?

For a written exam with few, if any, errors of fact or interpretation, an oral does little to provide additional insight regarding mastery of the program of study. This enlightened view makes the oral exam superfluous and is the reason several graduate schools make the oral optional. Find out if your program has this option. If it doesn't, why not discuss this with your chairperson as a possibility? The worst that can happen is that it can't be done.

When it is required, the primary purpose of the oral is to provide a way for elaboration on what has been written or for an explanation of a point or statement that is not completely clear or correct. The oral is scheduled, you meet with the committee, and the members ask whatever they want as it relates to your written exam.

Spend the time between the written and oral part reviewing what you have written. Review the exam by looking for areas of weakness. Think of yourself as a committee member preparing to take part in your oral exam. This person will quite likely review the written exam to determine areas of weakness or areas in which elaboration is needed. Do the same thing. This is particularly useful when a major part of a theory has been omitted or the work of one writer has been confused with that of another. Use the time to review the theories or literature supporting your written exam. Make notes in the margins of the written exam paper and be sure to bring this to the oral. Given that the examinee has written the material, most graduate schools allow this to be done. However, check the policy guidelines to be sure this is permitted.

Evaluating the Comp

The evaluation process is usually completed within a reasonable time period. Different graduate schools have different ways of evaluating the comp. Some use a point system and award a certain number of points for each correct answer. Others use letter grades or grade them as "pass" or "fail." Still others rank the exams in some other way. It is important to know when to expect the results and what type of results to expect. If you fail, what are your options for retaking the exam? What special considerations are provided for learning disabilities such as dyslexia? Discuss this before you take the exam.

If the exam is missed, the only option to make it up may be at the next scheduled administration. Obviously, this only delays the completion of the program and raises stress levels. Do everything possible to take the exam when it is offered. If it is absolutely impossible to take the exam when scheduled, check with your committee chair or department head to see what options are available.

Preparing for the Comprehensive Exam

Consult With Your Chair and Committee Members

When preparing for the comp, discuss any and all concerns with your chair or adviser. Being nervous or apprehensive about the written or oral part is a perfectly normal reaction. The committee chair should recognize this and may have some helpful suggestions.

Ask your chair or individual committee members if they can suggest ways to prepare for the exam. After all, it is virtually impossible to cover in detail everything that has been covered in courses over the past several years. Being concerned with time management, you want to make the best use of available time.

What is really desired is knowing which questions will be on the exam. Why not come out and discuss this? The worst that can happen is to be told nothing. More likely, some direction will be provided.

When seeking direction, listen carefully to what is being said. Don't be guilty of practicing selective hearing. If the committee member is saying that there will probably be a question or two on statistics, and for you this is not a strength, realize that there will probably be something on the exam that will pose a serious problem. Wishing it will go away won't help. Careful probing might even help determine what specific statistical techniques will be on the exam.

The same idea applies to any course that has presented problems in the past. If it is on the program of study, expect that a question related to the course will probably be on the comp. You know what was learned in a course regardless of the grade that was earned. If you haven't done well or are uncertain of what has been learned, it might be wise to audit the class again. Hire a tutor if it will help but don't think the tutor will teach everything that hasn't been learned before.

Review Course Notes and Textbooks

At the graduate level, trying to memorize the text or every note from every course is impossible. To try to do this is a waste of time. It can't be done.

When reviewing for the exam, class notes and marginal notes written in the text are especially valuable resources. Try to summarize the notes into a coherent, logical sequence or pattern. Some people have found that writing summaries is useful because the physical act of writing reinforces the thinking and review process. Write summaries on 3 × 5 cards. This makes them easy to review while riding on the bus, over lunch, or whenever there are a few free minutes.

Compare, Contrast, Analyze, Synthesize, and Integrate

When preparing for the comp, remember the following five key words: *compare, contrast, analyze, synthesize,* and *integrate.* These intellectual skills are intended outcomes of all graduate education. Furthermore, this is what frequently differentiates undergraduate from graduate education.

> *Compare:* to determine similarities
>
> *Contrast*: to determine differences
>
> *Analyze:* to determine the relationship of the parts
>
> *Synthesize:* to combine parts to make something new
>
> *Integrate:* to unite the parts forming a new whole

It is important to look for ways of comparing or contrasting sources of information. Comp questions call for more than a rehash of information presented in class. For example, in graduate school, it is common to assume that knowledge from the program of study has been mastered. Therefore, at the comp, expect to be asked to discuss the similarities and differences (i.e., compare and contrast) between and among the various ideas, thoughts, concepts, trends, and/or patterns that were presented in the course. Or expect to be asked to analyze the relationship of the various parts of a particular theory or how the course material can be applied (i.e., synthesized or integrated) within your own profession. Prepare accordingly.

Review Past Comprehensive Examinations

Some graduate schools provide copies of comp questions that have been used in past years for students to use for review and preparation. A typical comp question to an art historian might be as follows: "Compare and contrast Turner's and Canaletto's views

69

on landscape painting. How has each been influenced by the society in which he lived?" A philosophy major might be asked: "Elaborate on the differences and similarities between modern philosophers such as Descartes and Hume and existentialists such as Sartre. How have these schools of thought aided the development of your own philosophy?" A frequently asked comp question of an adult education major is the following: "Discuss the concept of 'andragogy.' Is it a philosophy or a practice? Analyze your own practice in light of this concept."

The list of comp questions will probably be extensive and overwhelming. There is no realistic way to write out adequate responses to all the questions on the list. No one is expected to do that, and no one should try. This is not the best use of time. These questions are provided to supplement preparation for the comp, not to supplant it. They serve to give an idea of the complexity and scope of past written exams.

A number of graduate programs provide complete copies not only of past questions but of responses as well. This can be particularly helpful if the writer of the exam is known. Speaking with that person will provide additional insights. Don't make the mistake of memorizing the responses of this person as there is no guarantee that the same questions will be asked again or that the answers are particularly good. Use the exam copies as an example, nothing more.

When reviewing prior comps, look at the content and form of the exam. Are there multiple parts to the question? What types of answers are called for? Comparison? Contrasting? Analysis? Synthesis? Integration? Are any general themes or topics discernible?

If your program does not provide past comp questions or exams, it is still possible to get examples. How? Speak with students or alumni who have recently completed the comps. Having gone through the process, they are frequently able to recall questions and discuss the problems they experienced. How did they feel sitting and writing the exam? What was the oral like? What tips or suggestions can they provide?

A word of caution is in order here as well. Keep in mind that individual opinions are being provided. Just because one person found the exam relatively easy does not mean that you also will find t easy. The reverse is also true. People learn and experience things differently.

Having access to past comps isn't always the blessing it may appear to be. Graduate programs that provide access to past comps can expect more from those taking the exam. More depth, precision, and reference to sources are generally expected.

Form Study Groups

A study group is a group of graduate students coming together for the purpose of preparing for the comprehensive exam. Study groups are usually more successful when comps are standardized or when they are scheduled at the same time. The most effective study groups are those that have been formed several months before the exam is given because the more time that is available the better the group will be able to prepare.

There is no format for a study group. Basically, the group looks at how best to prepare for the exam. Sometimes members who are particularly strong or have a particular interest in a subject or course act as tutors or discussion leaders for the rest of the group. They may deliver a mini-lecture or paper of some sort designed to stimulate thought and group discussion. Another variation is for each group member to prepare a series of questions or concerns on a particular topic for the group to consider. The success of any study group is intimately connected with the amount of support members provide one another. A supportive and nonthreatening environment is a critical part of the success of any support group.

When past comps are available, individual members can assume the task of reviewing them and reporting about both the form and the content of the questions. Group question analysis is often more effective than individual analysis because, when several individuals critique a prior comp question, it is inevitable that several different interpretations or rationales will be identified. This leads to more in-depth comparisons, synthesis, integration, and so on.

Some study groups have reviewed past exams to see if certain questions or certain types of questions have appeared more often than others. Others have identified the recurring themes, thoughts, ideas, or references that seem to regularly appear on the comps.

The study group might want to invite students who have recently completed the comps to speak with them. There is nothing more assuring than hearing from fellow students who have passed the exam. In addition to inviting successful graduate students to speak with the group, consider inviting faculty. Often faculty will provide much different insights.

Groups may wish to set up "mock" exams similar to those that may be in place in your program. This could mean responding in writing to questions either obtained from the graduate program files or prepared by fellow group members. Members of the group could act as the graduate committee at the oral exam. The examinees are expected to respond just as they would at the real thing. Following the exam, the group members offer suggestions to the responder regarding the quality and depth of the responses and provide other constructive criticism about the performance.

Without study groups, preparing for comps can be a lonely and anxious time. Study groups provide support and encouragement to members who are feeling discouraged or who are lacking confidence about the impending exam. Discussing this with someone who is also preparing for comps or who may be experiencing similar emotions may help eliminate the problem or reduce the anxiety. Whatever thoughts or suggestions are offered should be provided in a supportive atmosphere. The study group should not be used to ridicule weaker members or as a platform for the stronger members. The basis of a study group is to help each person recognize weaknesses, strengthen them, and successfully *pass* the comp.

Visit the Test Site

Some grad students worry about the actual test location. Sometimes this drains energy that could be given to reviewing for the exam. A simple suggestion is to visit the test site before the time of the exam. Seeing the site and realizing that it is usually nothing more than a regular classroom, lecture hall, or office can reduce if not eliminate this concern.

Taking the
Comprehensive Exam

Tips for the Written Exam

The actual act of writing responses to questions over a long period is physically demanding. It is not easy to write continually for several hours at a time. Many individuals find that their fingers begin to cramp from the pressure of holding the pencil or pen. Others experience back or neck pains from sitting in the same position for an extended period.

In Chapter 2, we discussed the relationship between physical condition and program completion. Keeping in good physical shape is also helpful in preparing to take the written comp. A physical conditioning program should be one in which your muscles are stretched and muscle tone developed.

It should also include practicing relaxation exercises. Particularly useful are those that can be used at any time such as taking deep breaths and exhaling slowly. Knowing appropriate relaxation techniques will enable you to apply them as needed when taking the written comp.

Some programs allow a dictionary, pens and pencils, and paper to be brought to the exam. Some will allow the use of books, notes, or whatever tools the student feels are needed to successfully complete the comp. It was not very long ago that calculators were banned from engineering exams. Now they are commonplace.

In this technological age, more and more graduate schools are allowing the use of computers when taking the comp. Others supply everything that is needed and will not allow anything to be brought into the exam room. It is important to know what may be brought into the test site and what is not allowed. Don't make any assumptions about this matter. Ask your chair or department head and be sure.

The RCOW Process. Let's assume it's the day of the exam. For some period, you have been preparing for the exam. The waiting has been stressful and has caused a certain degree of anxiety. But now the exam has been distributed and needs to be completed. Time is limited. Do not waste it.

Application of the *RCOW* (pronounced "are-cow") process can save time and facilitate completion of the exam. RCOW is the process of reading, comprehending, outlining, and writing.

THE RCOW PROCESS

1. *Reading*
2. *Comprehending*
3. *Outlining*
4. *Writing*

Begin by *reading* the exam, all of it. Don't write anything yet. Read the directions, each question, everything. Once everything has been read, try to *comprehend* what the questions are about. Think about what is being asked. What course does it relate to? What committee member is interested in this question? Whose concerns are reflected in the question?

At this point, think about which of the questions seems to be the easiest one to answer. Develop an *outline* as a response to this particular question. Include the names or sources of appropriate authors or references to be referred to in the response. Outline the entire response. Think about how much time may be needed to complete this question. Just because it is your strongest response, don't be too long answering it. Remember that all questions need to be answered during the allotted time for the exam.

After the outline is complete, start to *write*. Write in full sentences with correct grammar, punctuation, and syntax. Include an appropriate mix of your thoughts substantiated with references to the research and opinion of the leaders in the field. Be sure to answer all parts of the question. If the question contains multiple parts, as most graduate comp questions do, they are there for a reason and need to be answered. Be sure to provide comparisons if comparisons are asked for. Have you fully compared the landscapes of Turner with Canaletto? Did you remember to respond to the second part of the question?

Once the response to the first question is complete, go on to the next. Again, use the RCOW process of reading, comprehending, outlining, and writing. Do this for all the questions, keeping in mind the time allowed to complete the exam.

The RCOW process has helped many graduate students to complete exam questions not only on comps but also on course final exams. Use the process as needed.

Completing the Written Exam. Remember that this is a graduate comprehensive exam. It is an opportunity to demonstrate that you are "graduate" material and worthy of receiving a master's or doctoral degree. It also is an opportunity to demonstrate higher-order thinking and writing skills. Sloppy work does not convey a "graduate" image. At the comp, there are few acceptable excuses for poorly written responses. Be sure the responses are more than the reporting back of information gleaned in class. Remember to compare, contrast, analyze, synthesize, and integrate. Use the dictionary or computer spell-check.

Pace yourself. Use the RCOW process for each response. Also allow time to review initial responses to the questions. Review the response to ascertain that which may have been omitted. Revise the response accordingly. The time to spot omissions is before the exam is over, not after the exam has been handed in.

Tips for the Oral Exam

For many learners, this is the most stressful part of the comps because almost everyone has a certain amount of fear when speaking in front of a group. This fear is greater when the group is your graduate committee. They have the power to determine whether you receive the degree. Most learners enter this part of the exam feeling tense and anxious regardless of how much time has been spent reviewing notes and speaking with committee members or fellow graduate students.

```
┌─────────────────────────────────────────────────┐
│                                                   │
│         TIPS FOR TAKING THE ORAL EXAM             │
│                                                   │
│   1. Be prepared.                                 │
│   2. Use the "count to three" technique.          │
│   3. Paraphrase.                                  │
│   4. Be honest.                                   │
│   5. Listen carefully.                            │
│                                                   │
└─────────────────────────────────────────────────┘
```

As mentioned earlier in this chapter, not all master's degree programs have an oral exam. It is much more common in doctoral programs. If your program has an oral, here are some suggestions for preparing for and taking this part of the exam.

Be Prepared. Much of the fear associated with the oral concerns perceived rather than real issues. There are all sorts of rumors and horror stories about committee members who get their kicks out of making graduate students squirm. Although some really do enjoy this arrogant display of power, most committee members do not. Most are supportive rather than adversarial, but don't assume that this is always the case. You can control the situation as much as possible by being prepared, composed, and ready.

One way to prepare is to think of this time as a meeting of equals. The committee may have more knowledge and experience but you have just spent a great deal of time preparing for the comps and should be well prepared and well able to fully discuss the relevant theories, authorities, experts, and concepts of the field, particularly as they relate to the written comp.

Count to Three. A good way to maintain control at this difficult time is to use the tried-and-true "count to three" technique before speaking. This simply means mentally counting to three before responding. The technique is a subtle but effective control device because it gives the impression that the student is thinking before responding and that the answer may have some basis in the literature. Whether this is true or not is not important. The impression it gives is the main point. Mentally counting to three before responding gives the impression of being in control. It also provides "think time" to develop an answer. It is surprising how much the mind can come up with given those 3 extra seconds to work.

All too often, especially in times of stress, graduate students are so nervous that they jump in with a response before the question being asked has been fully developed. This can be devastating, particularly if the question being asked is not the question you answer. Using the "count to three" technique before responding helps to avoid this pitfall.

Paraphrase. Another strategy is to paraphrase the question before answering. This is based on the idea that people communicate in many different styles. For example, when some people begin to speak, they are not exactly sure of the point they want to make and begin with seemingly vague or unconnected statements. Their question or point is usually made clearer in their last few sentences. Others make their point at the beginning of their statement and then go on to elaborate. Frequently the elaboration is unclear or unnecessary and leads the listener to believe that another, different point is being made. The intent of the speaker to clarify the point or question through elaboration is not understood by the listener. The result is that the listener (the graduate student at the oral) doesn't know what point or question is really being asked.

To make matters worse, people usually respond to questions the same way they speak. If one's speaking pattern is to make the point and then to elaborate, the response pattern will probably be to respond to the first part of the speaker's statement. If one's speaking pattern is to make the point at the end of the statement, the response pattern probably will be the same. There is not much of a problem if the speaker (the committee member) speaks in a manner that corresponds to your response style. Real problems can occur at the oral when the speaker speaks in a manner different from your preferred response pattern. What can happen is that full communication does not take place; the student is not sure what is being asked but needs to respond. By paraphrasing the question before responding, the examinee is better able to maintain control of the situation, create more "think time" to develop a response, and, importantly, avoid answering the wrong question.

Paraphrasing is a very simple technique. In your own words, simply restate the question being asked. Examples of paraphrasing are these: "In other words, are you asking me to compare Descartes with Hume rather than to discuss Descartes?" or "I'm not exactly certain what you are asking but I think you wanted me to not only discuss 'andragogy' but also analyze my own office based on this concept. Is this what you want me to do?" The questioner will either agree and give you the opportunity to answer or will disagree and more clearly articulate the question or point. Either way, you have bought time to formulate a thoughtful response.

Be Honest. During the oral, it is important to be honest about what you know and what you don't know. Realize that there might well be several questions to which the answers are unknown to you. This is not unusual. Don't try to bluff the committee. This only serves to challenge them and they will usually come out the winner. A better approach would be to admit the uncertainty and demonstrate an awareness of how to get the answer by referring to appropriate sources or references for the answer. Another honest approach would be to pick a subsection of the answer that is known and focus on that.

Listen Carefully. Listen carefully to what is being asked at the oral. Some helpful tips are the following:

1. Eliminate distractions. Look directly at the speaker.
2. Control your emotions. Avoid prejudging and listen without interrupting.
3. Occasionally take notes. Writing it down helps you to concentrate on the question being asked.
4. Listen actively. Nod, smile; let your eyes show surprise, interest, delight, or concern.

Practice these techniques. For example, the next time a friend asks a question, make a conscious effort to look directly into his or her eyes the entire time the question is being asked. Nod appropriately. Try not to interrupt. After having given your response and the conversation is concluded, ask your friend for any reaction regarding your nonverbal action. How did your friend feel when you were looking directly into his or her eyes? What image did it project? Was there any reaction to the nodding of your head and not interrupting? How did you feel about this?

Take notes the next time you are being asked a question. Explain that this is being done as an aid to providing a full response. When the question and answer period is over, ask the person or group for reactions. Did they feel respected? Neglected? Did they feel you were sincerely interested in them? How did you feel? Did it give you time to think about a response? Did it help you to give a more accurate response?

As with any new technique, try it and determine how it works for you. The more these techniques are used, the more natural they become.

FIVE

The Proposal and the Thesis/Dissertation

About a year into my graduate program I remember coming home one night and telling my wife that I was dropping out. How could I be expected to complete the thesis with everything else going on in my life?

Her response was perfect. She listened, sympathized, and encouraged me to talk out the problem. Later that week, I made an appointment with my Chairperson and discussed it with him. I learned I wasn't alone. It is not easy to complete something as meaningful as a graduate degree.

Ted

The culminating experience in most graduate programs generally is referred to as a *thesis* at the master's level and a *dissertation* at the doctoral level. The proposal is a description of what the thesis or dissertation will contain.

Many, but not all, master's programs require a thesis. In those master's programs not requiring a thesis, a comprehensive examination (see Chapter 4) frequently serves to culminate the program. Almost every doctoral program requires a dissertation or its equivalent. It is difficult to settle on one word to describe the dissertation or its equivalent because some doctoral programs refer to it as a thesis and some master's programs call it a dissertation. Some graduate programs add to the confusion by calling it a research project or an applied research project regardless of whether it is at the master's or the doctoral level.

Each graduate program has its own policies and procedures for developing the proposal and completing the study. In the development of the proposal, most faculty are more concerned with the quality of the work rather than the number of pages. They will look to see if you have completely described the problem or topic, reviewed the literature as it relates to the topic, and presented appropriate methodology.

As has been suggested throughout this book, it is very important to know and follow program policies and procedures and to know the concerns of your adviser and committee. It is just as important to maintain as much control over the development of both the form and content of the proposal and the completed study as it is for any other part of the graduate program.

Developing the Proposal

Several books are available to assist with the development of the proposal and/or the thesis/dissertation (see the reference list at the end of the book). Many of these books suggest that there is a general pattern to follow when developing the proposal and that it is vital to be aware of this pattern as well as the requirements established by your graduate program.

Before writing anything, however, be sure to be familiar with the formal and informal procedures and processes in place in your program. Talk with current and former students, program administrators, and faculty. Review copies of completed proposals, theses, and dissertations on file in the main university or college library or in the department.

The Preproposal

Many graduate programs require the submission of a *preproposal* before permission is granted to develop the full proposal. Essentially, the preproposal is a shortened form of the proposal. Its purpose is to help with the development of the proposed topic or concept, identification of appropriate literature, and review of possible methodologies and/or data analysis techniques. For more details regarding the components of the proposal, see the section "Connecting the Proposal to the Thesis/Dissertation" later in this chapter.

A preproposal should fit on one page. The following is provided as a guide.

THE PREPROPOSAL

Statement of the Problem:

Objectives of the Study:

Importance or Significance of the Study:

Topics in the Literature to Be Reviewed:

Proposed Methodology:

Even if it is not required, it is a good idea to develop a preproposal because this encourages refinement of often vague ideas relating to the various parts of the proposed study. It also provides another opportunity to interact with your committee. By developing a preproposal, you are getting committee feedback prior to spending time and effort developing the proposal.

The Proposal

Some graduate programs have an unstructured process for the development of the proposal. This is to provide maximum flexibility and creativity and not to let form restrict the free flow of ideas. In these programs, students are encouraged to develop the topic, discuss and negotiate it with their chair and their committee, and refine it as needed.

In many other programs, a carefully structured process is in place regarding the development of the proposal. Guidelines and manuals are provided and students are expected to strictly adhere to them when developing proposals.

Ultimately, the proposal is approved by the committee and/or the graduate program and provides a skeletal understanding of what will be completed for the thesis or dissertation.

The Thesis/Dissertation

The most common outline for a thesis or dissertation is the following five-chapter format:

Chapter One: The Problem
Chapter Two: The Literature Review
Chapter Three: The Methodology
Chapter Four: Presentation and Analysis of the Data
Chapter Five: Summary, Conclusions, and Recommendations

The first chapter basically describes the problem or topic. A variety of subsections develop the topic and describe it in considerable detail. The second chapter contains a complete review of the literature that is directly and indirectly related to the problem or topic just described. The third chapter is a complete description of the methodology that will be used to respond to the problem. The fourth chapter contains the data that have been collected using the methodology just described. The fifth chapter completes the study by presenting conclusions and recommendations based on the data just presented.

Connecting the Proposal to the Thesis/Dissertation

Sharan Merriam and Edwin Simpson's book, *A Guide to Research for Teachers and Trainers of Adults* (1989, p. 181) developed a very helpful outline of a typical proposal that can be used as a guide for both the proposal and the first three chapters of the final report, as follows:

Proposal Outline

A. Introduction and Problem (Chapter One of the study)
   Introduction to the study
   Background to the study
   Statement of the problem (What is the problem or area of concern?)
   Purpose of the study (specific purposes and/or objectives)
   Rationale or theoretical basis for the study
   Hypotheses or questions to be answered
   Importance or significance of the study
   Definition of terms (operational definitions)
   Assumptions and limitations of the study
   Organization of the remainder of the study
B. Review of the Literature (Chapter Two)
   Introduction and organizational structure of the chapter
   Abbreviated review of pertinent literature, grouped around major topics or themes
C. Methodology (Chapter Three)
   Introduction (reviewing the purpose of the study)
   Description of methodology to be used (i.e., experimental, case study, historical)
   Design of the study (operationalization of variables)
   Sample and population or source of data
   Instrumentation

Data collection and other procedures

Data analysis (How do you expect to analyze the data once they are collected?)

It is helpful to think of the proposal in relation to the first three chapters of the completed study. Many graduate programs require that the proposal contain these three chapters. The proposal is a description of something to be done in the future. Therefore the proposal is written in the future tense. The final thesis or dissertation describes the completed project and is always written in the past tense. Thus it is not unusual that, with tense changes from future to past and other slight modifications, the proposal will become the first three chapters of the final study.

The purpose of the proposal is to describe in some detail the topic or problem, literature related to the topic, and methodology selected to respond to the topic. The topic is described in Chapter One of the proposal. Literature relevant to the topic is presented in Chapter Two and the appropriate methodology is presented in Chapter Three.

It might help to think of the proposal and the thesis/dissertation as analogous to a blueprint and the building of a house. The blueprint presents a skeletal picture of the house and provides a fairly good idea of what it will look like when it is built. The blueprint allows conferences with others and conceptual changes to be made prior to actually beginning the construction. So it is with the proposal. The proposal allows for the conceptualization of the topic, organization of the literature around the main ideas of the topic, and a discussion of the proposed methodology *prior* to conducting the study.

Chapter One:
The Problem

Chapter One of the proposal and the completed study are pretty much the same. Both fully describe the study problem or topic using subheadings similar to those indicated above. This can usually be done in about 10 to 12 double-spaced pages.

Introduction and Background

The "introduction" and "background" sections provide the reader with an overview of the topic or problem. It should be fairly brief (two to three pages) yet complete enough to give the reader a clear idea of the topic or idea. It should include a sufficient number of major references but not everything that has been said on the topic. The bulk of the literature review is presented in Chapter Two. These sections are intended to introduce the reader to the topic and should not be overwhelming.

For example, let's assume you are interested in the general topic of childcare in industry. After thinking about this topic, and talking about it with friends, colleagues, family, and faculty, it is decided that the focus is to determine whether childcare needs in your company (the XYZ corporation) are perceived differently by labor and management. In the introduction section, it is entirely appropriate to introduce the reader to the topic by discussing how the family has changed in the past two or three generations and how this has affected business. Authorities who have written on this subject or relevant statistical data to support the idea that effective childcare programs have affected business and industry are cited. After a page or two of this type of general introductory material, the reader should have a sense of the general nature of the problem of the study.

Next, more definite background information regarding childcare as it relates to industry is provided. Two or three sources supporting specific themes or ideas regarding childcare and industry are in order. Again, this section is not intended to be all-inclusive but should show that this is a topic worthy of further investigation or research.

Statement of the Problem

Follow this overview with a very brief (one to two paragraph) section referred to as the "statement of the problem." This is a succinct description of the topic of the study. It should end with a completion of the following sentence: "Therefore, the topic (or problem) of this study is. . . ." This sentence also can serve as the basis for the title of the study. The reader now should have a clear and unambiguous understanding of the problem or topic of the study.

Continuing with the childcare example, once the introductory and general background information has been provided, the "statement of the problem" section might end with this sentence: "Therefore, the topic of this study is to determine differences in perception by labor and management regarding childcare needs of the XYZ corporation."

Purpose or Objectives

Now that the topic has been introduced, background information provided, and problem succinctly stated, the proposal needs to describe the purpose(s) and/or objective(s) as they relate to the statement of the problem. This is provided in the "purpose of the study" section. What part or parts of the topic are of specific interest?

This section also is fairly brief (one to two pages) and clearly articulates the specific objectives or purposes of the study. This also serves to further focus the study. Objectives and purposes can be presented as a list or in narrative fashion.

An example for the XYZ corporation follows:

The specific objectives of this study are
1. to determine the childcare needs of XYZ corporation as perceived by labor,
2. to determine the childcare needs of XYZ corporation as perceived by management,
3. to compare differences in perceptions by labor and management regarding the childcare needs of the XYZ corporation.

Theoretical or Conceptual Framework

Next, the rationale or theoretical basis for the study is presented. This section may also be referred to as the "theoretical framework" or "conceptual framework" section. Its purpose is to develop and present an understanding of how the problem relates to a unified explanation of related ideas. This section further expounds on the topic by providing a summary of the major theories or research supporting, clarifying, refuting, or driving the notion that perceptions of labor and management may differ or may be perceived differently. It may also include references to similar studies in related areas and provide a rationale that conceptions of a variety of topics are frequently perceived differently by labor and management. These topics or themes are elaborated on more fully in Chapter Two: The Literature Review.

The theoretical framework is one of the most difficult sections to develop, but one that needs to be in the proposal as well as in the research study itself. It is difficult because it depends on an awareness of the value of theory in research. As it is almost impossible to clearly define theory, it is not difficult to see why this section is so hard to develop, let alone get faculty agreement on its relationship to your study.

When developing this section, remember that the place of theory in the study depends on what is known about the particular topic. When dealing with the general topic of motivation, for example, much available research has been synthesized, directed, or guided by theory. However, much less research has been conducted on adult motivation. Therefore there are many fewer theories to connect with the topic of adult motivation. The researcher's task is to decide, and ultimately get the committee to agree, that the study is testing a well-developed theory; clarifying, refining, or adding to a tentative theory; or seeking to develop a new theory.

When looking at the place of theory in our illustrative childcare example, this section would review theories relating to needs assessment and differences in perception, and provide a rationale for how they relate to the topic.

Hypotheses or
Questions to Be Answered

The "hypotheses or questions to be answered" section is the next stage in the problem identification, definition, and clarification process. Whether the study will have hypotheses or questions to be answered depends on the type of study being conducted. Broadly stated, research questions guide past- and present-oriented, descriptive, comparative, and/or evaluative studies such as case studies, historical studies, and simple correlational studies. Hypotheses are used in future-oriented, quantitative studies such as single or multiple group experiments.

Research questions are posed when one is working in areas that are relatively new or in which a great deal of prior research has not been conducted. Research questions serve to guide the research and provide an outline for presenting the data. When working in areas in which significant research has been done, it is more likely that hypotheses will be included as a hypothesis provides greater precision and predictive power. Similar to research questions, hypotheses also serve to provide a basic outline for presenting the data.

It is common for a research study to contain both questions and hypotheses. Again, this will depend on the topic of the study and the amount of research that has already been done. In our childcare example, one hypothesis with several parts would probably be used because a great deal of research has been done and theories produced in the areas of childcare needs and perceptual differences related to needs. For this example, the hypothesis might be as follows:

1. There are no significant differences in the childcare needs of XYZ corporation as perceived by labor and management.

The "importance or significance of the study" section asks why the study is being conducted. Why is it important? To whom is it important? How will the results of the study affect not only the XYZ corporation but other local corporations with childcare programs? What about other corporations in other parts of the state, region, or country? If several different perspectives can't be presented, a very basic question must be asked of the researcher: Why is this study being considered?

Definition of Terms

Within this section, operational definitions of major words or terms used in the study are provided. This section is included to aid the reader in understanding how specific terms are being used. Common, generally accepted terms associated with childcare programs in industry or with the research methodology being proposed are not routinely defined. Only uncommon terms or common ones being used in uncommon, unusual, or unconventional ways need to be defined.

For example, the childcare program in the XYZ corporation may be set up for "latchkey" children. As there is no commonly accepted definition for *latchkey*, this term needs to be defined as used in the study.

If one decides to use a variation of an accepted research methodology, this would be defined as well. Keep in mind, however, that some faculty prefer that anything related to the methodology be included in the methodology chapter. As always, fully discuss and negotiate any concerns with your chair or adviser and committee members.

Words or terms needing definitions are often found in the title of the study and in the purposes, objectives, rationale, hypotheses, and research questions sections. They should be briefly defined in Chapter One and may be elaborated on in the literature review section in Chapter Two.

In the XYZ corporation example, at least the following terms should be defined:

XYZ corporation

Childcare program in XYZ corporation

Labor

Management

Perception

Assumptions and Limitations

The purpose of the assumptions and limitations section of the proposal is difficult to clearly discuss because there is no general consensus regarding its function or what needs to be included. As always, once you have determined the assumptions and limitations appropriate to your study, discuss and negotiate them with your committee chair and committee members and come to an agreement regarding how this section relates to the study and what needs to be included.

Generally speaking, a section discussing the major assumptions underlying the study is required by most graduate schools. The researcher needs to determine what is a major assumption and what is not.

Many different types of assumptions may relate to the population or sample used in the study or may be concerned with subtle differences regarding cultures or societies. They may relate to age, sex, or other demographic variables among the study population. Assumptions may relate to the measures or to other aspects of the research design and methodology (e.g., Is it assumed that the personality test developed for the study is valid and adequately measures the personality characteristics that are central to the study?). Make the initial decisions about the importance of the assumptions and whether they need to be included in this section in consultation with your adviser.

Limitations provide another way to further clarify, quantify, delimit, or define certain aspects of the problem or topic that cannot easily be included in any of the sections discussed so far. The intent of the limitations section is to give special emphasis or to further clarify limiting factors that have not been discussed before.

Let's take another look at the childcare program of the XYZ corporation. In this program, let's say the "latchkey" kids make up 85% of the children in the program. Although this may have been discussed before, it should be mentioned here as a limitation as it possibly affects the generalizability or application of your results to other childcare programs in similar companies.

Organization of
the Remainder of the Study

The purpose of this section is to tell the reader what to expect in the remaining chapters. This alerts the reader to any deviation from that which is traditionally included in the remaining chapters. This section could be a paragraph such as the following:

> Chapter Two will discuss the appropriate literature related to the problem just described. Chapter Three will describe and discuss the research methodology selected to respond to the problem. Chapter Four will present and analyze the data collected using the methodology described in Chapter Three. The study will conclude with Chapter Five, which is a summary of conclusions drawn from the data presented in Chapter Four and will present recommendations for future research.

Chapter Two: The Literature Review

Chapter Two of the proposal and the thesis/dissertation is the literature review. In the proposal, it is frequently a brief review of pertinent literature grouped around major themes or topics. Some graduate programs require that it be completely developed in the proposal. Others may require an abbreviated review for the proposal and expect the fully developed review will be in place in the final document.

The literature review includes books, articles, interviews, or other print or nonprint sources of opinion, fact, or empirical data. The purpose of the literature review is to demonstrate that you are as current as anyone about what has been done related to the topic. A well-done literature review can establish you as an expert. At the very least, it should establish that you know a lot about your topic and have a good working knowledge of directly and indirectly related literature.

It is impossible to prescribe how many pages is appropriate for this chapter. This is determined by the topics and themes directly and indirectly related to the problem. It is not unusual for a completely developed Chapter Two to contain 50 to 75 pages.

Purposes of the Literature Review

1. To place the topic in a historical context

2. To provide for the assessment of previous studies
3. To justify selection of the topic
4. To assist in the selection of the research design and methodological procedures
5. To provide the theoretical framework

Establishing the Historical Context. It is fairly safe to say that no topic exists in isolation. When faced with making sense out of reams of computer-generated abstracts of literature relating to the topic, you may wish this were true, but it isn't. When writing about the topic, the need is to establish where it fits in relation to current and past studies. What aspects of the problem have been studied? When were the studies completed? What problems have been encountered? How have they been resolved? Looking at the historical context will also help to establish how this study is different from other studies and help to establish researcher credibility.

Assessing Previous Studies. The literature review also provides an assessment of previous studies as they relate to the topic. How reliable are the data and the analysis? How sound are the recommendations? How and why is the cited literature relevant to your topic?

Using the Five Ws to Assess Relevant Literature. The five "Ws" (who, what, where, when, and why) are helpful in determining the literature to be included or omitted.

When looking at the "who" aspect, consider the reputation of the author. How well known is this person? How many books, chapters, articles, and so on has this person published? How prestigious are the journals or publishers of this person's work? With the computer capabilities of most research libraries, it is relatively easy to run a search of the appropriate databases and determine how often the author and the articles have been cited.

Another dimension of "who" is to consider the population constituting the focus of the research. How were they sampled and what was the extent of the sampling? How does the "who" of this literature relate to your study?

Assess the literature in terms of "what" has been done as well as "what" are the results of that research. How can you use this literature? How does this relate to the proposed topic?

When looking at "where," most literature reflects at least one of the following four perspectives: local, regional, national, and international. Review the literature from the most relevant perspective(s). For example, when considering a topic relating to industrial psychology, looking at regional differences might be considered irrelevant as people learn through the same basic psychological processes in California as they do in New York. However, if the study is concerned with differences in attitudes, it is impossible to assume that the opinions of individuals in the West are the same as those in the East. The key to controlling this is to know the topic and to review the literature accordingly.

The same logic can be applied to reviewing literature with a local, national, or international flavor.

The purpose of reviewing literature from a "when" perspective is to determine the currency of the material. Research often runs in cycles. There are times when a great deal of research is done on a particular subject, interest subsides, then, for no apparent reason, it picks up again. Be sure to know if the literature being reviewed is in an up or down cycle.

There are several other reasons for needing to know when the research was done. It will help establish the historical basis for the research. It will determine if the research interest in this topic has waned. If this is so, the following question is a good one to ask: "Why am I interested in it?" Knowing when the study was done will also help determine if replicability is needed or warranted. Would a study completed in 1950 have the same results if completed on a similar population today?

Justification of the Topic

The last of the five "Ws" (why) not only helps to assess literature but also helps with the third purpose for doing a literature review—to justify the selection of the topic. Why was the study done? What problem was the researcher looking at? How does this problem relate to your study?

Aid in the Selection of Research Design

The fourth purpose of the literature review is to aid in the selection of the research design and methodological procedures. Reviewing the literature to determine what approaches have been used before, as well as their successes and failures, can save a great deal of time, effort, and money. Familiarity with other procedures can provide a base from which the researcher can select, modify, and create new designs useful in developing the proposal or study. Fortunate, indeed, would be the researcher of the XYZ corporation study who locates a research design or an evaluation instrument that parallels the study with the XYZ corporation.

Another word of caution is necessary here. Check to see if the material is copyrighted. If the questionnaire or instrument is copyrighted, permission from the copyright holder is needed prior to using it. This may involve the payment of a fee. In many cases, the copyright holder will grant permission to use the instrument free of charge. This is particularly true when the material is from a recently completed thesis or dissertation. Fellow students are quick to realize what others are going through and are thrilled and flattered that someone thinks enough of their work to ask permission to use it.

Generally, permission to use a research design is not needed because it is unlikely that every aspect of the copyrighted study will be exactly duplicated. More than likely, some or all of the variables will be changed. The copyright only prevents exact duplication.

If unsure whether or not to ask permission of the copyright holder, a good rule is to act on the side of caution and ask permission. Check this with your chair as well.

The Theoretical Framework

The fifth purpose of the literature review relates to the theoretical framework, which was discussed earlier in this chapter. Within the literature review chapter of the proposal, the material may have been summarized or briefly presented. In the final report, the literature review provides a strong theoretical framework for the study. For example, how do the different theories regarding perception relate to the XYZ corporation? On what basis were certain theories rejected as being irrelevant? In this section, the reader is provided with an increased understanding of the theoretical underpinnings as they relate to the study? In other words, what theory or theories are driving the study? How will they provide the basis for interpreting the data and presenting the implications of the findings?

A literature review that is logically organized, places the topic in a historical context, and presents a critical examination of the strengths and weaknesses of related research designs, methodologies, and theories of related studies will strengthen the claim that the topic is important and worthy of a research study at the master's or doctoral level. It will help justify the time and effort that will be spent in its completion. A carefully thought out and well-designed Chapter Two will also avoid a "So what, who cares?" response from your chair and your committee.

Chapter Three:
The Methodology

In this chapter, the design of the study and how it will respond to the problem so carefully articulated in Chapter One and supported with a thorough literature review in Chapter Two is described. This chapter clarifies each step of the research plan designed to respond to the topic clearly summarized in the statement of the problem section of Chapter One. This chapter can be fairly brief. It is not uncommon for Chapter Three to be 12 to 20 pages in length.

Introduction

Chapter Three begins with a brief introduction reviewing the purpose of the study. This helps to once again focus on the topic of the study. This section should describe the purpose using wording identical to that used to describe the purpose(s) in Chapter One. Exact repetition avoids any possibility of misleading the reader by subtly changing the meaning through the use of similar words.

Description of Methodology Selected

Next, describe the research methodology. How does it relate to the topic? Briefly describe the type of methodology you have elected to use (i.e., experimental, descriptive, historical, ex post facto, and so on) and any variations of the methodology (e.g., a modification of the Delphi technique or a quasi-experimental design).

It is important to remember that the nature of the problem determines the type of research that is best to use in a study. All too often a researcher is familiar with a certain type of design and wants to use that design regardless of the topic or problem. This is like putting the cart before the horse. An experimental design is used basically to test causal relationships between two or more variables concerned with "what will be" rather than "what is." This type of design, although neat and tidy, can't be used to obtain facts or to make judgments about existing situations and would not be a suitable design to use in the XYZ corporation study. A descriptive study would be more appropriate.

Design of the Study

The next item in Chapter Three is the "design of the study." In it, the operationalization of the variables is discussed. This section is generally rather brief. For a historical study, this section could discuss how the primary and secondary sources used were identified and/or obtained. In a simple experimental design, the operationalization of variables such as the control and experimental groups as well as the treatment would be discussed.

In the descriptive methodology most likely used in the XYZ company study, a discussion of how the surveys were executed; how, where, and when interviews were conducted; or the nature of any direct observations that may have been made is presented.

Sample and Population

Next comes a discussion of the "sample and population or source of data." In the XYZ study, the population is the XYZ labor and management force. The population for this study would, naturally, be drawn from the company. Ideally, the population would be the entire labor and management force, but if the population is too large or if it is otherwise impossible to obtain results from the entire population, a sample of the population can be used because a properly selected sample can provide meaningful information about the entire population.

In addition to discussing the population or sample used in the study, this section may discuss other appropriate sources of data obtained through various measures such as counting absences, new enrollments, observing various phenomena, conducting content analyses (the systemic analysis of communications), and objective testing.

Instrumentation

All instruments used in the study are discussed in this section. The purpose of a research instrument is to gather data. The choice of instruments selected to obtain the data is made after the methodology has been determined. Instruments may be verbal (e.g., structured interview forms used by an interviewer), paper and pencil (e.g., a written questionnaire), or more sophisticated electronic tests such as polygraph tests. Regardless of the type of instrument(s) used, it needs to be discussed in this section.

Quite possibly the literature reviewed in Chapter Two will have identified a variety of instruments appropriate for use in the study. In the proposal, the researcher should have discussed the instruments, determined their reliability (i.e., Are they accurate, stable, and will they repeatedly produce the same type of data?), their validity (i.e., To what extent do the instrument or instruments measure what they purport to measure?), their possible applicability to the study, and how they seemed to respond to the study purposes.

For those instruments actually used in the study, there is a need to present this information in the past tense as well as to present the data regarding the reliability and validity of the instruments. This usually can be obtained from the manuals that accompany the instruments.

Appropriate instruments for the XYZ study would be needs assessment instruments and ones that measure perception. Ideally, you would find instruments that have been used in childcare studies related to industry.

If the instruments that have been discovered are not appropriate for the purposes of the study, it will be necessary to develop instruments specifically for the study. As any research text will point out, this is not an easy process as it requires a great deal of additional time and effort to research possible test items, construct and revise questionnaires, conduct validation and reliability studies, and conduct pilot testing before the instrument is valid and reliable.

Reviews of hundreds of published tests and instruments of all sorts are in *The Eleventh Mental Measurements Yearbook,* published by the Buros Institute of Mental Measurements of the University of Nebraska. These volumes, published on an irregular basis since 1938, are a superb resource for any researcher (for the most recent version, see Kramer & Conoley, 1992). The reviews are accompanied by extensive bibliographies of research related to the use of the instruments. For obvious reasons, these volumes are a gold mine for any researcher and should be consulted when seeking information about available and appropriate instruments.

Data Collection
and Other Procedures

A discussion of the data collection procedures and techniques is the next to the last section that is included in Chapter Three. Within this section, the various procedures and techniques used in the study are presented. *Procedures* generally describe the way in which the data were gathered. *Techniques* refer to the ways in which the data were recorded.

As research follows a logical pattern, the research method selected for the study determines how the data will be collected. Data are usually collected in one of three ways: asking questions, observing, or testing. If the study is designed to identify causal relationships between two or more variables, for example, the data collection procedures would involve gathering quantifiable data from test scores, observations, ratings, or measurements.

In the XYZ corporation study, which is descriptive in nature, the data gathering procedures could involve the use of interviews, document analysis, comparisons, correlational studies, and/or evaluations.

Data Analysis

The plan for analyzing the data is the concluding section in the methodology chapter. Following the discussion of the procedures and techniques used to collect the data comes the discussion of the data analysis plan for the study. The purpose of this section is to demonstrate how the data analysis plan responds to the research questions or hypotheses. Few things are more frustrating to the researcher than to realize after data collection has been concluded that the data needed to test a specific hypothesis or research question were not collected or were not conducive to a particular type of analysis or statistical procedure. It is impossible to re-collect the data. For this reason, it is essential that the data analysis plan be well thought out and clearly connected to the problem statement, the purposes of the study, the research questions, and/or the hypotheses.

When appropriate, this section also discusses the descriptive and inferential statistical procedures that were used, how they were treated, and how the level of statistical significance used to guide the analysis was determined.

Chapter Four: Presentation and Analysis of the Data

Within Chapter Four are the presentation and analysis of the data. In the proposal, this chapter was only very briefly mentioned in the last section of Chapter One. The contents could not be fully discussed at that time as the study had not been done. There was no way of knowing what the data would look like, what trends might possibly emerge, how the research questions would be answered, or if the hypotheses would be accepted or rejected. The length of this chapter totally depends on the amount and depth of analysis being presented.

The purpose of Chapter Four is to present the findings. Data are presented in such a way that the reader will be able to draw independent conclusions from the data. If the data are presented correctly and fully, the conclusions of the reader should match those developed and presented by the researcher in this chapter.

Because there are considerable differences of opinion regarding the format of this chapter, it is once again suggested that you become familiar with graduate school and department policies and procedures and consult with your adviser and committee prior to developing and presenting your findings.

Findings are usually reported in a narrative format and supplemented with charts, figures, graphs, numbers, and so on. They may be grouped and presented in sections responsive to the research questions or hypotheses.

Regardless of how they are presented, all relevant data derived from the study should be reported in an objective, nonevaluative way, free from author bias or editorializing. This preserves the integrity of the data presentation and allows the reader to independently interpret the data and draw conclusions. It also helps separate fact from feelings. Although the researcher may be surprised, shocked, disappointed, or have any of a number of emotional reactions to the data, the data are reported objectively. If 23% of the population indicated something in a certain way and for some reason this is surprising to the researcher, it is reported factually (i.e., "Twenty-three percent of the population indicated. . . ."). Words or comments expressing surprise (i.e., "Only 23% of the population indicated. . . ." or "Isn't it surprising that 23% of the population indicated. . . ?") have no place in this section of the chapter. When reporting the findings, the words of Sergeant Joe Friday, from the old *Dragnet* television series—"Just the facts, Ma'am. Just the facts!"—are appropriate.

Generally, the factual presentation is kept separate from the inferences, interpretations, or other analytical treatment of the data. In some instances, data presentation and analysis are integrated throughout the chapter. The format of this chapter depends to a large extent on the nature of the data and the topic or problem of the study. If it is important for the reader to have all the data before conclusions can be drawn, then all the data are presented in one section followed by a section presenting the author's analysis or interpretation.

Chapter Five: Summary, Conclusions, and Recommendations

This chapter provides the summary, conclusions, and recommendations relating to the topic of the study. It begins with a summary of the entire study. It is a brief recap of the problem, the major themes on which the literature review was developed, the methodology, and the findings. This serves to refocus the reader on the topic of the study.

If conclusions were not drawn in Chapter Four, they are drawn here. The conclusions are one of the most important parts of the study because they provide partial responses to the research questions or provide the basis for accepting or rejecting the hypotheses.

It is essential that the findings and conclusions are tied to the theoretical framework described in Chapter One and elaborated on in Chapter Two. How do the findings and conclusions of the study relate to the theoretical framework? Are they supported by the theory? Do they seem to differ from similar studies using essentially the same theory?

If conclusions were drawn in Chapter Four, they need to be summarized and restated in this section. If conclusions were not made in Chapter Four, they need to be firmly presented in this chapter. Within this section, any additional insights or inspirations derived from the analysis are included.

The chapter ends with recommendations. There are usually two types of recommendations: those drawn directly from and supported by the data presented in the study (e.g., suggestions for changing policy, creating new programs, or implementing other findings relative to the XYZ corporation) and those peripherally related (e.g., suggestions for future research).

Implementation of recommendations directly related to the data may have an immediate impact on the problem or topic of the study. Recommendations relating to future research may complete the research cycle and serve to assist another researcher in responding to a similarly related problem or topic.

References and Appendixes

The thesis or dissertation ends with sections for references and appendixes. Essentially, the references provide the reader with a list of sources used in the study. The sources may have been directly quoted and so indicated in the text or they may have provided background information that contributed to the development of the topic or methodology. Appendixes include materials, such as earlier versions of questionnaires, cover letters sent to participants in the study, interview guides, results of pilot studies, or graphs, charts, tables, that provide more detailed information than that which is included in the text.

Concluding Thoughts

As discussed earlier, Chapter One of the proposal remains basically the same in the completed thesis or dissertation with the exception of tense changes from the future to the past.

Chapter Two may change from the proposal to the final report to include additional literature reflecting unexpected or unanticipated results derived from the data analysis. For example, let's assume that, in the XYZ corporation study, the data revealed a much greater difference in the perception of needs of the childcare program by female managers than the research would lead you to expect. When preparing the final report, it makes good sense to include any additional literature that might help to explain this. A more extensive literature search, using different descriptors, may reveal other studies with similar results. This additional literature is included in the final report as it provides a more complete basis for analyzing and interpreting the data.

In a well-designed proposal, Chapter Three will be a fairly complete outline for the conduct of the study. Except for the change of tense and other changes reflecting exactly what happened as opposed to what was predicted to happen, Chapter Three in the final report will look very similar to Chapter Three of the proposal.

SIX

The Defense

As an undergraduate, escape was my primary goal; memorize, regurgitate, and graduate was my motto. More schooling and another degree were not in my plans. Five years later I was back. I completed my master's and am now in a Ph.D. program. I have completed the first draft of my dissertation and am actually looking forward to the defense. Soon it will all be over.

I have long since decided that while education isn't exactly wasted on young undergraduates, it is much more fulfilling the second or third time around.

Craig

The thesis or dissertation is now complete. It has been accepted by your chair, the committee, the department, and the graduate school. You have worked hard to produce a quality document that not only adds to the knowledge base but also demonstrates your ability to produce a significant piece of research adhering to an accepted research design. You are now faced with "the defense."

Few things evoke more fear in graduate students than the defense. Horror stories are rampant of students struggling for years to complete the dissertation only to fail the defense: years of work wasted; hours and hours of work all for naught; a monumental waste of time, dollars, and effort; lives ruined; marriages destroyed; and on and on. It is absolutely amazing how much this has grown out of proportion!

It is rare that one fails the defense. Although it does occasionally happen, it is an infrequent occurrence and one that probably could, and probably should, have been avoided. In this chapter, we'll take a closer look at the purpose of the defense and present some techniques and strategies to make sure you are one of the vast majority who successfully pass the defense.

Understanding the Defense

Historically, the purpose of the defense was to assure all concerned that the work being defended was original, that the student was the author and was truly worthy of joining a very elite community of scholars. To accomplish these objectives, very formal examinations were scheduled. Often, to ensure the integrity of the process, visiting scholars not connected with the student or the university in any way were invited to participate in the examination process.

The preparation process took a great deal of time and energy. During this time, the haggard countenance of the individual was a dead giveaway that this person was preparing for the final defense.

Questions designed to elicit evidence of mastery of research design, literature related to the study, data analysis, or the ability to compare, contrast, analyze, synthesize, and integrate were considered fair game at many defenses. Questions were asked by all committee members often with little or no regard to the stress or tension they produced. When one examiner finished, the next began. The examinee was expected to answer every question correctly, thereby demonstrating a full command of both the research process and subject matter mastery.

There were other competing dynamics at work during the examination as well. Frequently, the members vied among themselves to impress the others on the committee. It became a matter of personal and professional pride for committee members to demonstrate depth of knowledge through obtuse questions related to obscure references. Discussions regarding minor points often took on major proportions.

It was no wonder that, in this context, horror stories of students completely falling apart during the exam or failing horribly were commonplace. The reality, however, was that most stories were more fiction than fact. Today, defenses are much more civilized.

This is not to say that failures are a thing of the past. Although it is uncommon, there are still enough examples of individuals failing their final defense to discourage any graduate student from treating this experience lightly or taking it for granted.

The truth is that if you have made it this far, failure is very unlikely. By this stage, grad students should be pretty well known by the school and their committee. It would be difficult to get to this point without being relatively sure of the anticipated result.

Most committee members want students to pass and join the ranks of scholars and practitioners who are leaders in the field. Few things give a major adviser, committee chair, or committee member a better feeling than the understanding that student success is due in some small measure to their efforts.

Preparing for the Defense

Many of the techniques and tips presented in Chapter 4 regarding preparation for the oral examination are also useful when preparing for the defense. It may be well to review them before proceeding with this section.

A Meeting With Peers

Remember to try to control as many aspects as possible of the defense process. To do this, psychologically view this meeting as a discussion among peers rather than as a very formal examination. The thesis or dissertation defense is probably the one time you do know more about the topic than your committee does. After all, you conducted the study, analyzed the data, and wrote the final report. You should be the most knowledgeable person available regarding the topic. Be proud of the study and don't be intimidated or let anyone belittle your work.

Know What Is in Your Study

While preparing for the defense, not only do you need to know the sources that have been cited, you also need to know everything about the content and format of the study. If it is in the thesis or dissertation, it is fair game for the defense.

Look carefully at each chapter. What are the various components of the chapters? Why are they included? What significance does each subhead have? Why were some subheads included and others omitted? Does the literature review provide a complete review of all themes or topics related to the topic? What is the theoretical framework that guides the study? Is the rationale for the methodology sound and well developed? Have all relevant data been presented? Are the conclusions data based? How are they related to the theoretical framework? How are they related to the statement of the problem, the purposes of the study, and the research questions or hypotheses? Are there any additional recommendations that could have been included?

Be sure to be able to explain any technical terms in clear, nontechnical language. This is especially important as it is likely that outside members of the committee may not understand the technical language and may ask questions in that regard. Don't use jargon and clichés when explaining terms. Also remember that form follows content and that there are no hard-and-fast rules about how many chapters are needed or about what belongs in each chapter. At this point, you need to be able to explain the study in terms of its particular content and format.

Play "devil's advocate" with yourself and identify as many weaknesses as possible. Be hard on yourself. Try to develop points counter to those stressed in your study. Know the arguments posed by those who may support a different theoretical framework.

Involve Others

One of the best ways to prepare for the defense is to ask friends, family, fellow students, and/or coworkers to raise any questions or concerns they may have about anything in your study. Often these people will provide fresh insight or raise concerns that can only be brought up by someone who knows little or nothing about the topic.

In Chapter 3, the roles and responsibilities of committee members were presented. As mentioned, it is common for one of the members (usually the dean's representative) to be appointed or selected from outside your field. When preparing for the defense, an advantage of involving a friend or colleague with little knowledge about your topic is that this person may raise similar kinds of questions as the dean's representative may raise.

The Mock Defense

Another good way to prepare is to have a "mock defense." This is a simulation activity wherein a panel of knowledgeable individuals (usually fellow grad students) are assembled and simulate a defense by acting as your committee. Many times the questions posed by fellow students are more difficult and demanding than those asked by the committee. The obvious advantage of a mock defense is that there is little to be lost and much to be gained through this experience.

Know Your Committee

Don't forget to consult with your chair about the defense. Get his or her thoughts about how defenses are conducted. What is the chair's role in this process? In some colleges, the chair consults extensively with the other committee members and the dean or graduate college representative to determine the questions or concerns that may be raised and attempts to screen them to ensure that they are directly related to the work being presented. Others care little about the questions that may be raised and facilitate the defense so that each committee member has ample time to raise each and every concern even if they have little relationship to your thesis or dissertation. It is always best to consult with your chair for any advice that can be given about the possible questions or concerns that may be raised, the communication style, and the research interests of the committee members, as well as any information that can be shared about the "outsiders" (the dean's representative or the graduate college representative) who may be present.

It also makes sense to find out as much as possible about the outside member of your committee. Check his or her reputation with other graduate students, faculty, and staff. Go to the library and review the publications of this person. When appropriate, weave this knowledge into your responses. Not only does this give the committee member a possible ego boost, it also helps you to remain in control as it demonstrates to the committee that you take the process seriously.

The worst-case scenario would be that your chair will share nothing. In most cases, careful and tactful probing will produce valuable information about the concerns of the committee members and the process and the content of the defense.

Don't overlook this opportunity to consult directly with the other committee members as another means of preparing for the defense. Use the same type of careful and tactful probing to solicit their advice. Again, you can lose nothing and usually will gain a great deal.

Consult With Recent Graduates

Check with others who have recently been through a defense in your department. What were their experiences? What professors asked the most difficult questions? Who asked the easy ones? How helpful or how much of a problem was Professor X, who also happens to be on your committee?

Regardless of who is asked and how reliable this person is, remember that this person is not you and he or she has not produced your study. All anyone can do is to provide advice based on personal experience. It is your job to process it to help in your preparation. Don't take advice as gospel and fail to fully prepare simply because a fellow graduate student said that Professor X didn't ask "that type of question." Maybe that was so in his or her defense, but it doesn't mean that it will be so for you. It is much better to overprepare and not have certain questions asked than to underprepare and wish that you had done a better job of preparation.

Attend Other Defenses

The length of a defense may vary anywhere from 45 minutes to a few hours. There is no set way in which it is conducted. In some graduate colleges, the process is described quite clearly in policy guidelines, but in others, the process is developed by the department or committee.

In some graduate colleges, the defense is open to all and is publicized as a learning opportunity for the community of scholars. In others, it is an activity closed to all but the student and the committee.

If they are available, take the opportunity to attend as many defenses as possible. Try to attend those where your chair and other committee members may be observed in action. How do they seem to react to the student? Are they overly concerned with impressing others with their knowledge? Are they supportive of the student? What types of questions do they ask? Do they seem to have a consistent pattern of raising questions or concerns?

As a courtesy, check with the student to see if your presence would be a problem at the defense. When the defense is open to all, it creates more stress for most students regardless of how well they have prepared. Anything to help a fellow student at this time is always appreciated.

In some cases, your presence might not be welcomed. The only way to know for certain is to ask the person involved.

What to Do at the Defense

Play the Name Game

Prepare carefully for the defense. Just like the oral exam, this means knowing every source or reference in the study. This is also called "playing the name game." Be absolutely sure you know who said what and why it was said. If a particular name or reference has been included, it is your responsibility to know what the author is saying and how it relates to your work.

Often, graduate students blithely include in their study all the sources or references that happen to be cited in a related article or research report. If the author thought it was important, it probably was. What is not known for certain is the motivation of the author. All that is known is that the author of the article or report included the additional sources.

Including sources identified in this manner can lead to trouble in the defense particularly if a committee member happens to be familiar with the additional sources. It is embarrassing to be totally unfamiliar with an author or reference cited in your study. Avoid this by spending the extra needed time to become familiar with all sources. Although this will surely require additional time, it is worth it.

How to Respond to Questions

First, remember the tips you used when you took the oral part of your comprehensive exam. Again, this is discussed in Chapter 4.

Let's assume that everything suggested in this chapter to prepare for the defense has been done. The introductions are over and the first question has been asked. What do you do? Again, controlling the process as much as possible is the key to success.

One way to maintain control is to think of yourself as a witness on the stand at a trial. Lawyers prepare witnesses by telling them to answer the question honestly but to volunteer nothing more. The rationale is to force the other side to be very clear about what is being asked. At the defense, your role is not to sidestep the issue but to provide only what is being asked for and not to give more information than is required.

Although the defense should not be viewed as an adversarial relationship between you and your committee, answering the question in as few words as possible, but as fully as possible, makes good sense. This forces the committee members to more clearly articulate points they want elaborated.

By volunteering more than is called for, you may provide a committee member with additional information to develop another question. Recognize that the committee members are quite capable of developing their own questions and that you are possibly hurting yourself by raising concerns they may not have considered.

This is not to suggest answering questions in monosyllabic statements. Quite the contrary: Answer the question as fully as possible and with as much conviction as possible. Demonstrate confidence and self-assurance.

Even with the most extensive preparation, it is likely that you will be asked about something with which you are not familiar. Committees expect this and are generally more receptive to an honest response rather than one in which you try to bluff your way through it.

I Don't Know but . . . A better way to respond to a question to which the answer is unknown might be something like this: "I'm not certain of the answer to that question but here is my thinking on it" or "I'm not sure but here's how I would go about getting the information. I would go to such and such a book and look it up or I might do a search of the literature using descriptors such as____ and____."

Used judiciously, the "I don't know but . . ." approach actually can be positive because it can demonstrate that you are in charge, in control, and not intimidated.

Refer Back to Your Study. Another useful strategy is to remember that questions may be asked that are clearly answered in the thesis or dissertation. A frequent reaction is to think the questioner has not read the study, otherwise that question would not have been asked. Maybe this is so, but don't second-guess the reason for the question. Respond to it. Carefully handled, this situation can provide another opportunity to demonstrate that you are "in charge."

For example, assume that a question has been asked that is directly answered by a chart that appears in Chapter Four of the study. Being very familiar with your work, you know it is in that chapter. As part of your response, skillfully direct the attention of the committee to the right section or page of the study where the answer appears, then proceed to answer the question. Tactfully handled, this demonstrates obvious familiarity with your work and your concern for not embarrassing the committee member in front of colleagues by pointing out that he or she has perhaps not fully read the work or may have missed the obvious answer to the question.

The Decision

Sooner or later, the defense will be over. At the end of the defense, it is quite common for the chair to ask that you excuse yourself from the proceedings to give the committee an opportunity to discuss the defense and make a decision. When defenses are open learning events, the committee may seclude itself or conduct this part of the defense in private. This is usually the time when a formal vote is taken and decisions are made.

If all goes well, the committee reconvenes, offers its congratulations, and begins the process of welcoming you to the community of scholars. If the results are not positive, you will be told of the results and the available options.

As a result of substantive and editorial concerns raised at the defense, it is common for the committee to request that additional changes be made in the thesis or dissertation. When these have been made and accepted by the committee, the chair processes the final papers. Then you are done and are ready to graduate. Congratulations!

SEVEN

Now What?

I don't think anything prepared me for the impact graduate school would have on various aspects of my life—most particularly regarding my relationship with my spouse.

Only after a rather serious discussion with my committee chair and a group of fellow students did I even become aware of how my relationship with my husband was being shortchanged. I realized that sharing allowed him to feel included in the process. That helped the two of us get through some pretty rough spots.

Mary Ann

Completion of a graduate degree puts you in a rather elite group of college graduates. You have worked hard and should feel proud of yourself. All the work, time, and effort have paid off. Objectives have been set and accomplished. Although the hard part is over, a few things still need to be considered.

Binding Your Thesis or Dissertation

Even if it is not required by your university, consider having several copies of your thesis or dissertation bound with a hard cover and

117

embossed with the title and your name on the spine and on the front cover. With the preponderance of computers and desktop publishing, it is quite easy to revise the format of your study so it looks as though it were a printed book. Binding provides a way of permanently preserving your study. A gift of a bound copy is also a meaningful way to thank your chair and members for their help. It is a particularly significant way to show your appreciation to "significant others," such as parents, your spouse, or others without whose help the degree might not have been completed.

Library binding companies provide this service and are usually listed in the yellow pages of the local phone directory. Many commercial duplicating services also provide a binding service. Public libraries are always having books rebound and can provide the names and addresses of local companies that may provide this service. The college or university library or bookstore may also be able to provide leads for this service.

Copyrighting Your Work

Many graduate programs require that all studies be copyrighted. This is for your protection in the unlikely event that someone may claim your study as his or her own. Information regarding copyrighting your material can be obtained from the following agency:

> Registrar of Copyright
> Copyright Office
> Library of Congress
> Washington, DC 20559
> Telephone (202) 707-3000

The amended Copyright Act of 1976 grants owners of a copyright the sole and exclusive right to do or to allow others to reproduce all or part of the work, to distribute copies, to prepare new versions based on the original work, and to perform and display the work publicly. Copyright protection covers both published and unpublished works, that is, your thesis or dissertation. Even if you are not required to copyright your work, do it anyway. It is a relatively inexpensive process and will provide protection for your work.

In some instances, the outcome of a thesis or dissertation is a new product, idea, or discovery that may be worth money. By copyrighting your work, it will be protected to the fullest extent of the law.

In 1991 the National Association of College Stores (NACS), Inc., and the Association of American Publishers produced and copyrighted a booklet titled *Questions and Answers on Copyright for the Campus Community*. This publication can be obtained by writing to the association:

National Association of College Stores, Inc.
500 East Loraine Street
Oberlin, OH 44074-1295

Publishing Your Work

Everyone who has ever completed a thesis or dissertation wants to have it published. Very few ever do. Only three of my doctoral advisees and one of my master's advisees have been successful in having their work published as a book. In all cases, they spent more than a year following graduation working to revise their work into formats that were acceptable to their publishers.

It is much more common for studies to be reworked into an article that is published by professional or scholarly journals. In this regard, several of my advisees, at both the master's and the doctoral levels, have had articles published based on their graduate work.

It is important to the field for graduate students who have produced a particularly good thesis or dissertation to disseminate the results of their work. The study abstract is a good starting point for the development of an article. However, before completely developing the article, review the professional journals to determine acceptable formats. Most journals or scholarly publications provide guidelines for authors upon request.

Your committee chair or committee members are another source of assistance in developing the article and getting it published.

119

However, whenever working with one or more of your committee on the development of a book or article based on your study, or with any coauthor, consider the following procedural and ethical questions:

1. Who is the primary author, you or your adviser?
2. How do you determine if your adviser should receive recognition as a coauthor?
3. How will you split royalties?

The answers to these questions are based on considerations such as the amount of work expended on idea development, research, identification and review of the literature, and other logistical concerns. If your major adviser has made the primary contribution to the development of the work, then he or she legitimately should be primary author. However, if you have done the majority of the work, you should be listed as primary author. If publishing is an intended outcome of your work, answers to these questions should be determined as early as possible.

The three authors of *Teaching and Learning Basic Skills: A Guide for Adult Basic Education and Developmental Education Programs* (1984) are myself and two former doctoral advisees. In 1980, I received a grant to produce a manual for teachers of adults in Arizona. The grant provided funds for two research assistants. I interviewed several candidates and hired two doctoral students in my department. Under my direction, we researched the needs of teachers of adults in Arizona, reviewed existing literature including material from other states, and developed, field-tested, and evaluated drafts of material responsive to these needs. The ultimate product was a field-tested manual for teachers of adults in Arizona.

From the beginning, it was my desire to publish the results of our work in the form of appropriate articles or a book. I discussed this with each of the candidates interviewed for the research assistantships. One of the first things we did when the team was finalized was discuss how to operationalize this. Among other things, we decided that, as I had conceived and developed the idea, directed the project, written much of the material, and reviewed everything that was produced, I should be primary author. We also determined a procedure for listing who would be the second and third authors and how royalties would be split.

Once the manual was produced, our obligation to the funding source was complete. As we planned, I sent letters to various publishers. Eventually, Teachers College Press published a greatly modified version of the manual. When the book was published, there were no hurt feelings or bruised egos because the three of us had raised questions and developed solutions right from the start of the project. This created an atmosphere of mutual trust and respect. The research assistants found a way to finance their graduate degrees and also experienced their first publication. I was able to record another professionally significant entry on my résumé.

University Microfilms, Inc. (UMI)

No discussion about publishing would be complete without the mention of University Microfilms, Inc. (UMI), one of the world's largest and most widely used bibliographic information files. The UMI Dissertation Services program accepts all dissertations for publication and provides widespread access to your work.

More information can be obtained from them directly:

University Microfilms Inc. (UMI)
300 North Zeeb Road
P.O. Box 1346
Ann Arbor, MI 48106-1346
1-800-521-0600

Making Up Lost "Quality Time"

Now that you have earned a master's or doctoral degree, a major question is this: "What do I do with all the time I used to spend working on my degree?" One of the first things to do is to become "reacquainted" with your family. In most families, many sacrifices have been made for you to complete your graduate degree. Spouses have spent many hours without your company when you have been in class, preparing for an exam, writing your thesis, or researching your dissertation. Probably there were any number of times your spouse or mate surely wanted to go to a movie, go out with friends, go to dinner, or do anything other than stay home and watch TV and keep quiet.

Although it is true that you, alone, completed your graduate degree, it probably could not have been done without help, particularly from those you live with. Ideally, you have kept these very important people as involved as possible. As mentioned in Chapter 1, many changes and sacrifices were needed for you to complete this degree. Now that you are done, some show of appreciation is in order. Whether appreciation is demonstrated in the form of something tangible, such as an inscribed bound copy of your thesis or dissertation or other gift of some sort, or in the expression of deeply felt feelings, it is strongly encouraged that action be taken to show just how much the efforts of all concerned are appreciated.

Realize, too, the sacrifices of your children. They may well have wanted to spend part of the weekend with you but had to give it up for you to have the needed study time. How many evenings did they do without their mommy or daddy because you were in class or at the library? Maybe they had to be out of the house so you could have quiet when you were working on your computer. Don't forget, it is their home too.

A classic case in point is that of the 4-year-old, who upon being told that mommy had finished her degree said, "Does that mean I don't have to go to the zoo every weekend anymore and now you can be a real mommy?" How much was said in that sentence?

Commencement

A wonderful way to bring the family together and to formally celebrate completion of the graduate school experience is to attend commencement and to have a graduation party. This is a formal and highly appropriate way to bring closure to life as a graduate student.

In most colleges and universities, the relatively few graduate degrees being awarded enables special attention to be given to the recipients of these degrees. Many graduate colleges stage an impressive ceremony of "hooding" master's and doctoral degree holders. Each individual name is called out, the proud recipients walk across the stage in full academic regalia, accept the congratulations of the president and chancel party, receive the diploma, and accept the accolades of professors, family, friends, and colleagues.

Following the ceremony, families take pictures and bask in the glory of the graduates. It is a time for joy and one that shouldn't be missed. Commencement provides an opportunity for those special people to share in your happiness. Give yourself and them this opportunity. Go to commencement.

Using the Title "Doctor"

Since royalty was eliminated in the United States, the title "Doctor" has been seen by many to be the closest thing the United States has to royalty. Power and prestige are often associated with a person holding this title. It is amazing how many receptionists will put through a call from *Dr.* Jones with no screening but will interrogate *Mr.* Jones before putting the call through.

Society frequently views the holder of a doctorate with awe and with a certain amount of deference and respect. Some holders of the doctorate feel the title gives them credibility and will use it professionally but will not use it socially. Others will use it both professionally and socially. Many holders of a doctoral degree insist on being referred to as Dr. _____ by everyone. Although this may be considered by some to be presumptuous, it is not wrong because there is no correct response regarding when to use the title and when not to. Each individual needs to consider his or her situation and his or her own reactions to the use of the title.

Avoiding Emotional Letdowns

Don't be surprised if an emotional letdown accompanies the completion of the degree. This is very common. Ideally, with the degree have come additional knowledge and wisdom. However, you are still basically the same person you were when you started.

An emotional letdown is easy to understand, particularly for those who have completed a doctorate. The title of the old song sung by Peggy Lee, "Is That All There Is?" is particularly poignant at this time. You have spent much of your life going to school. First you completed primary school and high school. Then you went to college and completed your bachelor's degree. Graduate school was probably always in the back of your mind. When everything was in place, you were accepted into graduate school and began work on the degree. A lot of time, money, and energy were devoted to this. Many sacrifices were made by you and others. The constant stress of completing and controlling the process has been a part of life for a considerable period. Now this is gone. Although it is good to be relieved of this pressure, its release can create a letdown.

Although many expect sirens to wail and fireworks to emblazon the sky when they complete the degree, this won't happen. Life returns to normal. You have really only just begun and now need to put the new knowledge to work.

One way to avoid the letdown is to plan to use the time formerly devoted to graduate work for other scholarly activity such as writing the book or article discussed in this chapter (see the previous section "Publishing Your Work"). How about taking some of that time and using it to implement the plans or recommendations that were suggested in your study? After all, who knows more about the rationale behind the recommendations? Or use this time to become more involved with a hobby or to read all those mystery books that were put on the shelf until after graduation. Take the family on a vacation. Visit friends you haven't seen for a while. Have a good time.

Put Your Degree to Work

There are many real and perceived changes concurrent with the completion of a graduate degree. Using myself as an example, within 1 year after having earned both my master's and my doctorate, I had secured new professional positions and was earning significantly more money.

Eric, Gene, and Patrice are three former advisees who negotiated well and benefited greatly from the completion of their degrees. They used their degrees wisely.

As part of a grant we were working on, Eric received an assistantship to develop a series of staff development training modules. He did his job well and produced all that was asked of him. More important, he asked many questions and learned a great deal about the process of researching and writing grants.

After graduation, he secured a university position and proceeded to write grants to finance his own research interests. He became so good that others began to ask for his help in writing grants. Within a few years, Eric wrote and published a book about grant writing. He developed and offered a series of grant writing workshops around the country and is in great demand as a consultant. He is now a tenured, full professor and well respected in his field.

Gene was a middle-aged business person with an M.B.A. and a successful small business when he entered graduate school to work on his Ph.D. He had been quite interested in the personal well-being of his employees and had spent a great deal of time talking with them. Gene realized that what he really liked best was being able to help people with their problems.

After completing necessary prerequisite courses, he was admitted to a doctoral program in psychology. Through the required core courses, he gained a strong theoretical foundation in psychology. Gene realized he needed more than the usual field experiences to gain additional counseling experience. Being used to negotiating, he arranged not one but three internships in local area mental health facilities. He clearly demonstrated an ability to combine compassion with practicality. Upon graduation, he was hired by the mental health agency in which he had completed his last internship and successfully made the transition from business person to counselor.

Patrice had a bachelor's degree and was working as an administrative assistant in a small, midwestern hospital. It did not take her long to realize that she needed a master's if she was going to experience any career advancement.

She entered a master's degree program with a concentration in human resources. A practicum was required as part of her degree program. Patrice negotiated this experience so she could develop a sorely needed personnel policy manual for her hospital. Once this was developed, with the approval of her chairperson she also developed, field-tested, and evaluated the manual. The entire process formed the basis of her thesis—a case study describing the development, field-testing, and evaluation of a personnel manual for a small, midwestern hospital.

Shortly after Patrice graduated, the hospital human resource coordinator retired. Because of her graduate work, Patrice was the logical person to be offered the position. She quickly accepted it and is now making a major contribution in her chosen profession.

Eric, Gene, and Patrice are three of many thousands of success stories from individuals like you who have made the decision to complete a graduate degree. Their lives have changed; their futures are more secure. Like countless others, they were fearful of the unknown when they began but they used their motivation, desire, and ability to complete their degrees. They did it! They negotiated. They persevered. So can you. Good luck negotiating graduate school.

References

Council of Graduate Schools. (1991). *The role and nature of the doctoral dissertation: A policy statement.* Washington, DC: Author.

Cross, K. P. (1982). *Adults as learners.* San Francisco: Jossey-Bass.

Kramer, J. J., & Conoley, J. L. (1992). *The eleventh mental measurements yearbook.* Lincoln: University of Nebraska, Buros Institute of Mental Measurements.

Merriam, S. B., & Simpson, E. L. (1989). *A guide to research for teachers and trainers of adults* (updated ed.). Malabar, FL: Robert E. Krieger.

National Association of College Stores, Inc. (1991). *Questions and answers on copyright for the campus community.* Oberlin, OH: Author.

Rossman, M. H., Fisk, E., & Roehl, J. (1984). *Teaching and learning basic skills: A guide for adult basic education and developmental education programs.* New York: Teachers College Press.

General Style Guides

*Achtert, W. S., & Gibaldi, J. (1992). *The MLA style manual.* New York: Modern Language Association of America.

NOTE: An asterisk (*) before the name indicates a particularly useful book.

*American Psychological Association. (1994). *Publication manual of the American Psychological Association* (4th ed.). Washington, DC: Author.

*Campbell, W. G., & Ballou, S. V. (1990). *Form and style: Theses, reports, term papers* (8th ed.). Boston: Houghton Mifflin.

Chicago guide to preparing electronic manuscripts for authors and publishers. (1987). Chicago: University of Chicago Press.

The Chicago manual of style (14th ed.). (1993). Chicago: University of Chicago Press.

Howell, J. B. (1983). *Style manuals of the English-speaking world: A guide.* Phoenix, AZ: Oryx.

*Miller, C., & Swift, K. (1988). *The handbook of nonsexist writing.* New York: Harper & Row.

*Modern Language Association of America. (1988). *MLA handbook for writers of research papers, theses, and dissertations* (3rd ed.). New York: Author.

Strunk, W., & White, E. B. (1979). *The elements of style* (3rd ed.). New York: Macmillan.

*Turabian, K. L. (1987). *A manual for writers of term papers, theses, and dissertations* (5th rev. ed.). Chicago: University of Chicago Press.

U.S. Government Printing Office. (1987). *Style manual* (rev. ed.). Washington, DC: Author.

Webster's standard American style manual. (1985). Springfield, MA: Merriam-Webster.

Guides to Writing a Proposal, Thesis, Dissertation, or Research Paper

Allen, G. R. (1973). *Graduate students' guide to theses and dissertations.* San Francisco: Jossey-Bass.

*Balian, E. S. (1994). *The graduate research guidebook: A practical approach to doctoral/masters research.* Lanham, MD: University Press of America.

Barzun, J., & Graff, H. (1985). *The modern researcher* (4th ed.). Orlando, FL: Harcourt Brace Jovanovich.

*Behling, J. H. (1984). *Guidelines for preparing the research proposal* (rev. ed.). Lanham, MD: University of America Press.

*Castetter, W. B., & Heisler, R. S. (1977). *Developing and defending a dissertation proposal.* Philadelphia: University of Pennsylvania, Graduate School of Education, Center for Field Studies.

Davinson, D. (1977). *Theses and dissertations: As information sources.* Hamden, CT: Linnet.

Davis, G. B., & Parker, C. (1979). *Writing the doctoral dissertation: A systematic approach.* Woodbury, NY: Barron's Educational Services.

Dissertation handbook: Preparing and submitting your doctoral dissertation. (1990). Ann Arbor: University of Michigan, Horace H. Rackham School of Graduate Studies.

Gardner, D. C., & Beatty, G. J. (1980). *Dissertation proposal cookbook.* Springfield, IL: Charles C Thomas.

*Gates, J. K. (1994). *Guide to the use of libraries and information sources* (7th ed.). New York: McGraw-Hill.

Lawler, E. E. III, & Associates. (1985). *Doing research that is useful for theory and practice.* San Francisco: Jossey-Bass.

Leedy, P. D. (1993). *Practical research: Planning and design* (5th ed.). New York: Macmillan.

*Lincoln Y. S., & Guba, E. G. (1985). *Naturalistic inquiry.* Beverly Hills, CA: Sage.

*Locke, L. F., Spirduso, W. W., & Silverman, F. J. (1993). *Proposals that work: A guide for planning dissertations and grant proposals* (3rd ed.). Newbury Park, CA: Sage.

*Madsen, D. (1992). *Successful dissertations and theses* (2nd ed.). San Francisco: Jossey-Bass.

Mauch, J. E., & Birch, J. W. (1989). *Guide to successful thesis and dissertation* (2nd ed.). New York: Marcel Dekker.

Miller, J. I., & Taylor, B. J. (1987). *The thesis writer's handbook: A complete one-source guide for writers of research papers.* West Linn, OR: Alcove.

*Norusis, M. J. (1988). *The SPSS guide to data analysis for SPSS/PC.* Chicago: SPSS, Inc.

*Powers, R. L. (1992). *Getting what you came for: The smart student's guide to earning a master's or a Ph.D.* New York: Noonday.

*Sheehy, E. P. (Ed.). (1986). *Guide to reference books* (10th ed.). Chicago: American Library Association.

*Simon, M., & Francis, J. B. (1992). *The dissertation cookbook.* Dubuque, IA: Kendall Hunt.

Sternberg, D. (1981). *How to complete and survive a doctoral dissertation.* New York: St. Martin.

*Stock, M. (1985). *A practical guide to graduate research*. New York: McGraw-Hill.

Van Til, W. (1986). *Writing for professional publication* (2nd ed.). Newton, MA: Allyn & Bacon.

*Walker, M. (1993). *Writing research papers: A Norton guide* (3rd ed.). New York: Norton.

*Weidenborner, S., & Caruso, D. (1994). *Writing research papers: A guide to the process* (4th ed.). New York: St. Martin.

Williams, J. M. (1990). *Style: Toward clarity and grace*. Chicago: University of Chicago Press.

Researching and Writing in the Disciplines

American Chemical Society. (1986). *The ACS style guide: A manual for authors and editors*. Washington, DC: Author.

American Institute of Biological Sciences. (1978). *Council of Biological Editors style manual: A guide for authors, editors, and publishers in the biological sciences* (4th ed.). Arlington, VA: Author.

American Institute of Physics. (1978). *Style manual for guidance in the preparation of papers for journals published by the American Institute of Physics* (3rd ed.). New York: American Institute of Physics.

American Medical Association. (1966). *Style book and editorial manual* (4th ed.). Chicago: Author.

Barrass, R. (1978). *Students must write: A guide to better writing for scientists, engineers, and students*. New York: Wiley.

*Becker, H. S. (1986). *Writing for social scientists: How to start and finish your thesis, book or article*. Chicago: University of Chicago Press.

Blalock, H. M. (1985). *Causal models in the social sciences*. Hawthorne, NY: Aldine.

Brownlee, K. A. (1984). *Statistical theory and methodology: In science and engineering* (2nd ed.). New York: Wiley.

Campbell, D. T. (1988). *Methodology and epistemology for social science: Selected papers* (E. S. Overman, Ed.). Chicago: University of Chicago Press.

*Kerlinger, F. N. (1986). *Foundations of behavioral research* (3rd ed.). New York: Holt, Rinehart & Winston.

References

*Krathwohl, D. R. (1988). *How to prepare a research proposal for funding and dissertations in the social sciences.* Syracuse, NY: Syracuse University Press.

Kronick, D. A. (1985). *The literature of the life sciences: Reading, writing, research.* Philadelphia: ISI [Institute for Scientific Information] Press.

Long, T. J., Convey, J. J., & Chwalek, A. R. (1985). *Completing dissertations in behavioral sciences and education: A systematic guide for graduate students.* San Francisco: Jossey-Bass.

*Morgan, J. L. (1983). *Beyond method: Strategies for social research.* Beverly Hills, CA: Sage.

Remington, R., & Schork, M. A. (1985). *Statistics with applications in the biological and health sciences* (2nd ed.). Englewood Cliffs, NJ: Prentice Hall.

*Smith, R. (1990). *Graduate research: A guide for students in the sciences* (2nd ed.). New York: Plenum.

About the Author

Mark H. Rossman has been advising graduate students for his entire academic career. He is Professor and former Chair of Education at Walden University and National Specialization Lecturer at Nova Southeastern University. He has chaired doctoral dissertation committees and master's thesis committees for more than 120 graduates. He has been Professor of Education and Director of Graduate Studies at Ottawa University, Associate Professor of Adult Learning and Head of the Department of Higher & Adult Education at Arizona State University, and Assistant Professor and Head of Adult Education at the University of Massachusetts. Among his honors and awards are the Distinguished Service Award from the Commission on Adult Basic Education, a Certificate of Commendation from the Mountain Plains Adult Education Association, a Fellowship from the Salzberg Seminar in American Studies, recognition as a Visiting Scholar from the University of Kent in Canterbury, England, and a Master of Humane Letters honorary degree. He is the author or coauthor of 7 books, 10 evaluative reports, and 35 chapters or articles. He has produced one film, nine self-contained instructional modules, and two audiovisual tape curriculum units. He has served on the editorial boards of four professional associations and has presented 58 papers in 11 states and four foreign countries.